the soccer method

ATTACKING
DOWN THE CENTER

Henk Mariman

**Library of Congress
Cataloging - in - Publication Data**

the Soccer Method
Book 3 - Attacking Down the Center
by Henk Mariman

ISBN-13: 978-1-59164-105-6
ISBN-10: 1-59164-105-5
Library of Congress Control Number: 2006903028
© 2006

Editing
Bryan R. Beaver

Translation from Dutch
Dave Brandt

Printed by
Data Reproductions
Auburn, Michigan

Reedswain Publishing
562 Ridge Road
Spring City, PA 19475
www. reedswain.com
info@reedswain.com

Contents

Introduction

The coaching of young soccer players requires a lot of sensitivity. In particular, they must be allowed to retain their individuality. The impact of individual quality is even greater in the attacking line than in defense and midfield. Attackers must be able to develop their individual qualities and skill to the full. The coach must ensure that they can do so, without suppressing their individuality. In practice, this means that the coach's starting point is the player's technical, tactical, physical and mental characteristics. A fast attacker who makes good forward runs and demonstrates strength on the ball must be encouraged to develop these characteristics. In addition he must learn to play with his back to the goal. The coach must help him to develop his individual characteristics, but must also help him to develop the typical skills needed in his position. Attackers must also learn how to recognize whether there is space to run with the ball and take the initiative. Attackers who are skilled at taking the ball past an opponent or at making runs must be protected. Such players are rare.

In brief
When a coach focuses on how the striker and the withdrawn striker combine, or how the two attackers and the other players combine, he must take three important aspects into account:
- The individuality of the players.
- The typical qualities needed to play as a striker or withdrawn striker.
- The space for individual runs and initiative.

THE CONTENTS OF THIS BOOK

After reading this book, a coach should be able to incorporate central attacking play into his training sessions. I have divided the central attacking play module into six sections.

Section 1: All typical aspects of central attacking play that need to be worked on ("work items") are collected here. I have distilled the most important work items from the numerous soccer matches I have watched between teams of young players.

In **section 2**, I define the tasks and functions of the total team, the lines of the team (defense, midfield, attack) and the specific positions (based on a 1-3-4-3 team formation).

In **section 3**, I describe all the aims associated with the creation of goal-scoring chances. These aims are aligned to the chosen playing system. There are explanations of the typical aspects that need to be worked on.

Section 4 deals with the ball skills needed to create chances. These techniques are linked to coaching points and practice drills.

Young soccer players can be coached in 2 ways. The players can learn about the aims of the game, and they can learn about the specific soccer problems revealed by analyzing real matches. In **section 5**, I explain more about this.

Section 6 contains specific drills. The level of these drills is adapted to the different age groups.

Work Items

WORK ITEMS

In recent years I have watched a lot of youth soccer matches at various levels. I have identified the most important aspects of central attacking play that need to be worked on and divided them into two categories.

- Insight-related aspects
- Technique-related aspects

INSIGHT-RELATED ASPECTS

There is no interplay between the striker (9) and the withdrawn striker (10)

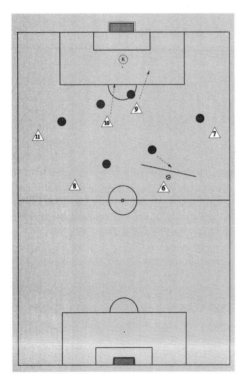

The striker and the withdrawn striker each play for themselves. There is no interplay.

The strikers play too deep.

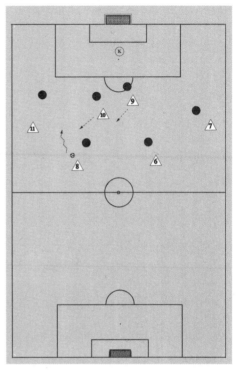

Both strikers do not get far enough forward, or they come toward the ball too soon. Too little space is created and there are too few opportunities to pass the ball forward.

"Good strikers are rare. You sometimes have to be satisfied with what is available – a mobile front man, a player with ball skills, a target man who can hold the ball and lay it off, a goal thief like Gerd Müller, a deceptively slow player or a fast blinkered one. It's all a question of taste."

Jan Mulder

The attackers make no forward runs.

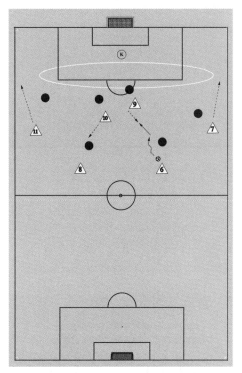

The striker (9) and the withdrawn striker (10) tend to want the ball played to their feet. There are therefore no opportunities to play the ball into the attacking zone for them to run onto.

The striker (9) moves out to the flank too often.

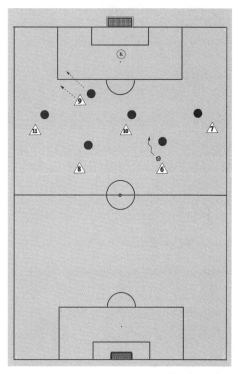

When a striker moves out to the flank too often, his wingers have less space. He is also available less often in the center. This sometimes enables the opposing team to organize more easily.

Neither striker is accessible.

The ball is played around in a team's own half. Neither striker is accessible in the center. The opposing team can stay organized without any difficulty.

> "Henry likes to move out to the left and then call for the ball."
>
> *Tonny Bruin Slot*
> *Assistant coach of Ajax Amsterdam*

The striker (9) reacts too late to the run by the withdrawn striker (10).

The withdrawn striker falls back too deep.

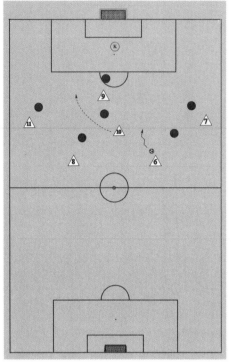

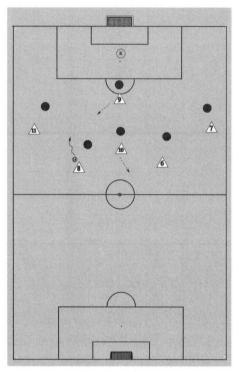

The withdrawn striker takes the initiative and makes a forward run off the ball. This opens up an opportunities for the striker. The striker reacts too late, so nothing is gained from the forward run.

The withdrawn striker has the task of supporting the striker. This includes making overlapping runs. If he falls back too deep, his attacking contribution is reduced.

The starting point is the player's individuality.

The striker (9) or the withdrawn striker (10) moves too soon.

The attackers come too close to the ball.

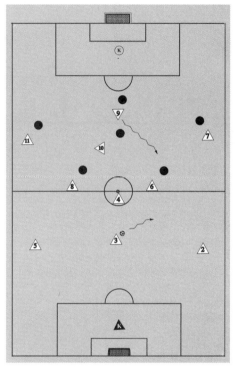

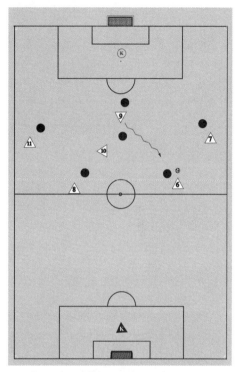

It is important that the attackers recognize the right moment to run into position to receive the ball. Some attackers start their too soon and therefore get out of position or close down space.

Good timing is of the essence when running into position to receive the ball. Attackers who run into position too soon often get too close to the ball or are stationary when they receive it. Opponents can intercept the ball more easily.

Both players always go directly toward the ball.

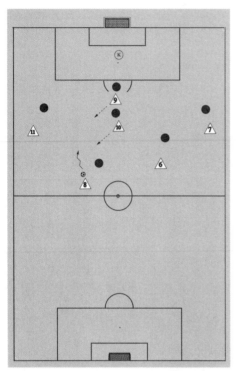

Neither player is taking account of what the other does. Both of them move toward the ball. They therefore take both their markers toward the ball. The chance of successful combination play is therefore smaller.

"You have to shoot at the goal to score."

Johan Cruijff

The ball is laid back too often.

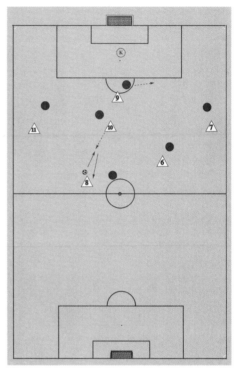

By laying the ball back too often, the players refuse to accept responsibility. Attackers must be able to make runs with the ball. Laying the ball back too often is not good for the development of a young player.

The two attackers take up positions close to each other.

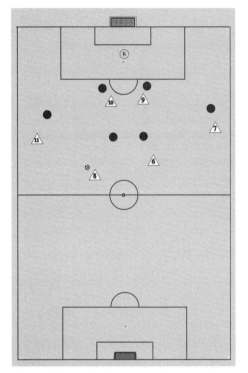

The striker (9) and the withdrawn striker (10) are too close to each other. The opposition can defend more easily.

The attackers are not opportunistic enough.

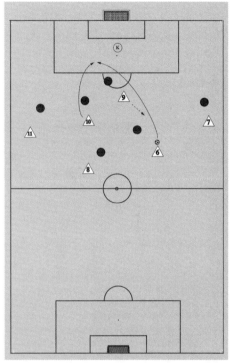

Stereotyped build-up plays make life easy for defenders. Sometimes an opportunistic action can create a breakthrough. Young players must be willing to do the unexpected.

The players are too obvious when they make themselves available to receive a pass.

The players should not be too stereotyped when they present themselves for a pass.

"Check away toward the goal and then back toward the ball. If your opponent is too close, take him forward with you and then suddenly check back toward the ball. This is how you make space for yourself."

Simon Tahamata

The ball is played to the flank too late.
When the ball is played through the center, this often creates more space on the flank, This should be exploited quickly.

When the ball is played to the striker (9) who has no support from his teammates, the team immediately loses possession.

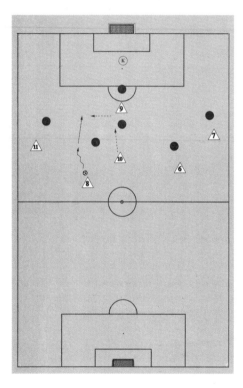

The striker receives the ball but there are no teammates nearby to support him. He therefore makes a run with the ball and immediately loses the ball. The defenders and the midfielders are moving forward and are therefore vulnerable to a counterattack.

Too few runs are made with ball.

The attackers rarely take the initiative. Too few attackers dare to accept the challenge of a 1v1 situation.

TECHNIQUE-RELATED ASPECTS

The lay-off

- *The ball is not laid off in such a way that the receiver can play it immediately.*

Receiving the ball

- *The player gets the ball under his body when he receives it*
- *He fails to control the ball with his first touch*
- *He fails to control the ball in such a way that he can immediately move with it in the desired direction*

Tasks and functions

TASKS AND FUNCTIONS

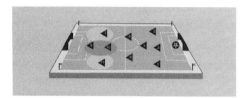

I have chosen a 1-3-4-3 system, to which I have linked a way of playing. Within each system and the associated way of playing, there are tasks and functions for the team as a whole, the lines (defense, midfield, attack) and the individual positions. The tasks and functions in this description are totally oriented to the development of young soccer players.

Age plays a key role here. The tasks and functions differ for each age group. The tasks and functions described here are aimed at 15 to 18-year-olds. Coaches of other age groups can integrate those tasks and functions that are suitable for their own players.

By describing the tasks and functions, I am not putting the players in a straightjacket. Attacking play should not be stereotyped. Chances are created by making runs, taking initiatives and interchanging positions. These elements cannot be described in terms of tasks and functions. The tasks and functions described here are more a framework for the coach than a target to be achieved. In the coaching of attacking play, the individual contribution of the player is the starting point.

More specific tips for each age category are given in section 5. The emphasis is on the roles of the players who are chiefly involved in attacking play.

"It is better to devise 10 clear slogans or impose a limited number of tasks. This creates clarity and structure for the players."

Willy Reynders

TASKS FOR THE WHOLE TEAM (ATTACKING)

- Make the playing area as large as possible (length and width).
- Don't stand too close together or too far apart.
- Try to create dangerous situations in the opposing team's penalty area as quickly as possible, without neglecting the philosophy of retaining the ball.
- Create opportunities to play passes forward (to run on to) or to feet.
- Take up good positions in front of the goal when the ball is crossed.

TASKS FOR THE INDIVIDUAL LINES (ATTACKING)

Defensive line
- No unnecessary loss of possession in your own half.
- Circulate the ball quickly.
- Try to switch the play as quickly as possible.
- Try to play the ball forward as quickly as possible.
- Try to play the ball to teammates in space.
- Take up good positions relative to your teammates.
- Use the space well relative to the opposing team's strikers.
- Communicate.

Midfield line
- Read the game.
- Take up positions that allow the ball to be played forward into attacking zones, or take up positions where you can receive the ball.
- Support your strikers.
- Fast play (one-touch play – good ball control – take up good positions).
- Don't run forward too early.
- Take over each other's positions.
- Create dangerous situations as quickly as possible by:
  - Shooting at the goal
  - Playing the ball into the space between the defenders and the goalkeeper
  - Playing the ball forward to the striker/wingers

- Playing the ball forward to the withdrawn striker
- Switching the play from one flank to the other
- Taking up a position on the edge of the penalty area for a cross

Attacking line

- Good cooperation between the striker and the withdrawn striker.
- Take up positions that allow the ball to be played forward into attacking zones.
- Good movement (run toward the ball, then check away again).
- Keep the playing area as large as possible (wingers stay on the flank).
- Vary your runs into space so they are not predictable. Create space for individual runs with the ball.
- Be aware of the third man.
- Don't move toward the ball too early.
- Take up good positions in front of the goal for a cross.
- Remember that the aim is to create chances and score goals.

TASKS PER POSITION (ATTACKING)

Right and left backs (2 and 5)

- Fan out toward the flanks.
- Be ready to react quickly if possession is lost.
- Be aware of what is happening in the attacking zone and play the ball to your attackers if you can.
- Look out for opportunities to pass the ball forward into attacking zones.
- Support the winger.
- Keep possession if build-up down the flank is not possible.
- Communicate with the players on the flank.
- Try to overlap the winger if the game situation allows it.

Midfielders (6 and 8)

- Try to create opportunities to pass the ball forward into attacking zones.
- Support the strikers.
- Do not make a forward run too soon.
- Keep the play under control.

- Focus on creating chances.
- Good positional play relative to the other players.
- Take up a position on the edge of the penalty area for a cross
- Don't close down the space in front of you by moving forward into it.
- Switch the ball from the center of the field to the winger.
- Try to overlap the winger if the game situation allows it.
- Create space for individual runs with the ball.

The withdrawn striker (10)

- Alternate supporting and overlapping roles.
- Be available to receive a lay-off from the striker.
- Don't take up positions too far forward.
- Good positional play relative to the other players.
- Be available.
- Use the space created by the striker.
- Get into scoring positions.
- Remember that the aim is to score goals.
- Be aware of the third man.
- Take up good positions in front of the goal for a cross.

The striker (9)

- Remember that the aim is to score goals.
- Read the build-up play.
- Try to get into scoring positions.
- Be available.
- Play forcefully in the attacking zone.
- Don't just lay the ball off; make runs with the ball too.
- Make space for the other players.
- Be aware of the third man.
- Take up good positions in front of the goal.

The wingers (7 and 11)

- Be available to receive the ball on the flank.
- Make runs with the ball or join in combination plays with the aim of crossing the ball.
- Time your runs with the ball well.
- Take up good positions in front of the goal when the ball is crossed from the other flank.
- Be aware of the situation in front of the goal before you cross the ball.
- Remember that the aim is to create chances and score goals.

The aims of the game

ATTACKING DOWN THE CENTER

The game of soccer can be broken down into 3 situations: own team in possession, opposing team in possession, and change of possession. Possession can in turn be broken down into 2 phases:

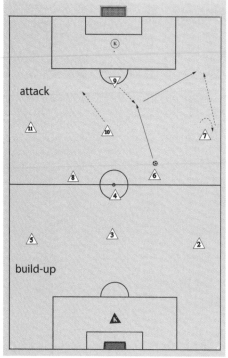

The build-up is the preparation for the attack. The players try to get the ball forward purposefully and efficiently. Build-up play from the back takes place in the team's own half and around the center circle.

> *The aims of the game must be translated into practice to promote the individual development of the players rather than just to get a result.*

Attacking is all about creating chances in the opposing team's half of the field. The players try to create a scoring chance and score. The attacking play module deals specifically with the striker (9) and the withdrawn striker (10) and how they combine with the other attackers, the midfielders and the defenders.

To achieve this, we must look at attacking play in detail. In this section I explain the basics of attacking play in a manner that furthers the players' development.

I discuss the most common aims and principles of attacking play.

The aims of attacking play

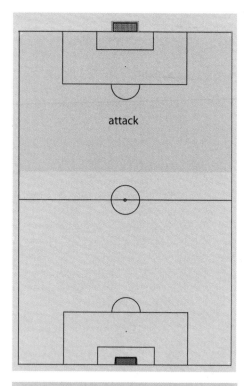

Aims:
- To create dangerous situations in the opposing team's penalty area.
- To score goals.

By:
- Individual runs with the ball, combination play, forward passes and shots at goal.
- Crossing the ball.

The decisive phases of attacking play

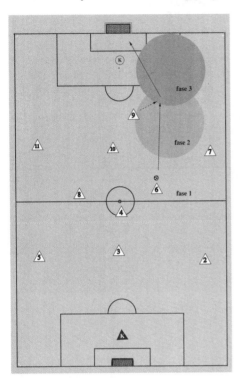

Phase 1: Creating a chance
Phase 2: The final pass – individual run – shot at goal.
Phase 3: Scoring

The execution of these 3 phases determines the efficiency of the wing play.

General starting points

The following general starting points are the basis of attacking play. Depending on the age group, the coach can integrate these points partly or fully.

Options for creating chances

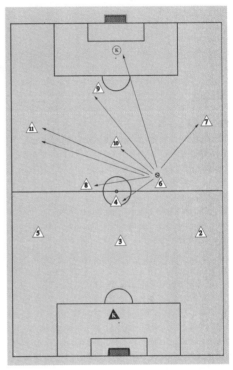

For attacking play, the rule is "want to get the ball into the attacking zone, be aware of the situation in the attacking zone, and play the ball into attacking zone whenever possible." Success depends on acting quickly. Pressure to play the ball forward must not lead to playing it forward at every opportunity and neglecting the basic principles of playing soccer. The players must not simply rely on blind chance. There is a hierarchy of choices:

- Create danger in front of the opposing team's goal
  - Shoot at the goal
  - Run with ball

- Play the ball forward into space for the attackers
    - Through the center
    - Via the flank
- Play the ball forward to an attacker's feet
    - To the striker (9)
    - To the withdrawn striker (10)
- Play the ball square
- Play the back

Choice 1

In the opposing team's half, creating danger in front of the goal is the main priority. If the attacker can create danger by making a run or shooting, this is the logical first choice.

Choice 2

A forward pass is often only possible immediately after winning possession or when the opposing players have a lapse of concentration. Creating a chance through the center (shorter route to the goal) is preferable to passing the ball out to the wing. A team that threatens down the center will also find more space on the flank.

Choice 3

A pass to feet down the center is usually aimed at the attacker in the most advanced position. Usually this is the striker (9), but it may also be a player who has taken over his position. Some strikers make a forward run off the ball too soon during the build-up phase and are therefore not accessible. In a 1-3-4-3 system it is important for the striker to serve as a target man during the build-up phase. Other players (the withdrawn striker, or the right or left midfielder) can make overlapping runs off the ball. After laying the ball off, the striker can take up a position for the finishing phase.

The ball can also be played to the withdrawn striker (10). In view of the fact that he is further from the opposing team's goal, I regard this as the second choice.

15 to 18-year-olds: Insight into the available choices is an important aspect at this age. The players must be able to recognize the importance of getting the ball into the attacking zone.

10 to 14-year-olds: The importance of getting the ball forward provides structure for young soccer players in this age group. Simple instructions, emphasizing attacking play, are important. The coach must take account of the players' need to have freedom of movement and not use the hierarchy of choices as a straightjacket.

> "A soccer player can have well developed intuition without necessarily having good tactical insight. Insight is conscious, intuition is unconscious. Insight is more to do with seeing and understanding the tactical situation and reading the game.."
>
> *Louis van Gaal*

Interplay between the striker (9) and the withdrawn striker (10)

Efficient interplay between the striker and the withdrawn striker in relation to the other attackers and the midfielders can considerably increase the success of attacking play. Such interplay is mainly about creating and using space.

> *Runs off the ball by the withdrawn striker are crucial.*

Example:
The striker can see the withdrawn striker's run and adjust his play accordingly. The two can agree on the following:

- If the striker comes toward the ball, the withdrawn striker makes a forward run.
- If the shadow striker comes toward the ball, the striker stays forward or makes a forward run (diagram 2).

15 to 18-year-olds: At this age, the two players can be encouraged to cooperate, although care must be taken not to suppress their individuality. An attacker who is able to adjust his play to a teammate or an opponent has a head start in the process of developing into an adult soccer player.

10 to 14 year-olds: The youngest players are not always able to cope with attempts to structure their play. There is a danger that their freedom of movement will be restricted. At this age it is better to leave the players a lot of space and simply give them tasks that will further their development.

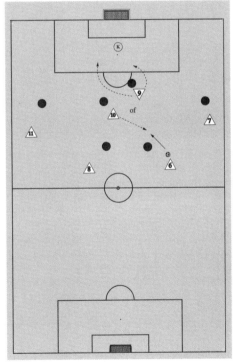

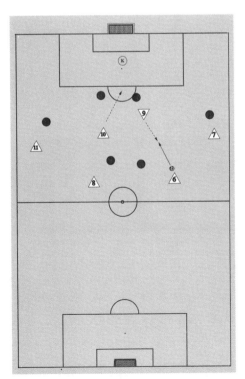

Swapping positions

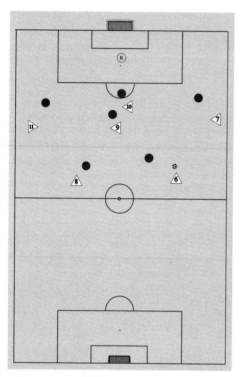

Each attacker is able to swap positions with the other and take over his tasks. This manner of playing makes life more difficult for opponents and introduces an element of surprise.

15 to 18-year-olds: At this age, swapping positions and tasks is a basic requirement. Developing this ability gives the players a head start when in the transition to adult soccer.

10 to 14 year-olds: At this age it is preferable for the players to learn the basic requirements of a specific position. It is better for a 10 or 11 year-old to play for a few weeks in a specific position (e.g. shadow striker) and then for a few weeks in another position (e.g. striker).

Taking up positions

It is important that the striker (9) and the withdrawn striker (10) do not take up positions level with each other. They should take up positions behind and to one side of each other (diagrams 3 and 4). They can then create space for each other and have more combination options. When they are on the same level, they are easier to defend against (diagram 1).

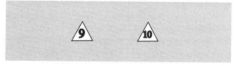

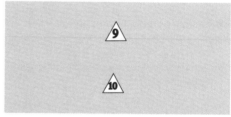

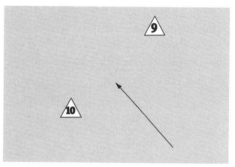

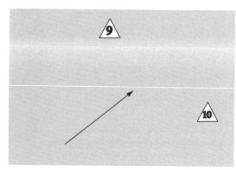

15 to 18-year-olds: Being able to take up positions relative to each other is a key aspect, alongside the development of an individual style of play.

10 to 14 year-olds: 10 and 11-year-olds are just starting with 11v11. In effect, their development process has just started. In this phase it is important that the players have enough space to develop. The coach can give them tips that will further their development and must never put them in a straightjacket.

The striker's action radius

It is important that the striker (9) restricts himself to a limited action radius. Strikers who move out to the flanks often close down other players' space. The striker should restrict his action radius to the center of the field.

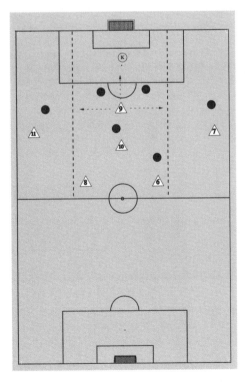

The withdrawn striker's action radius

The withdrawn striker (10) has a wider action radius. In youth soccer it is important that he stays close to the striker. When the withdrawn striker drops too far back (behind the midfielders 6 and 8), his supporting and overlapping roles become more difficult to carry out.

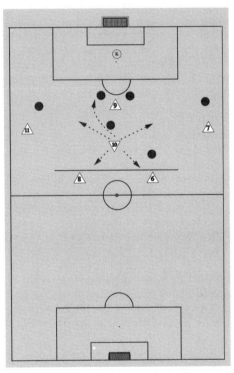

15 to 18-year-olds: At this age the withdrawn striker's play depends on the opposing team's manner of playing and the strengths and weaknesses of his own and the opposing team.

10 to 14 year-olds: The tips given to the players must not hamper their development process.

The role of the striker (9) and withdrawn striker (10) in attacking play

The striker as a target player

In the build-up phase, the striker in a 1-3-4-3 system is mainly a target player. Some strikers elect to make forward runs in this phase. This often makes them inaccessible and reduces the effectiveness of the playing system. A striker is primarily a target player who lays the ball off. In view of his position (with his back to the opposing team's goal) and the fact that he is closely marked, there is little likelihood that he will be able to make a successful a run with the ball.

Playing the ball to the striker has the following advantages:
- The striker is the player who is closest to the opposing team's goal.
- Playing the ball to the striker opens up opportunities for others. The withdrawn striker or the midfielders can make forward runs.
- The striker is in the center of the field. This means that he can move in all directions.

This philosophy does not mean that there are doubts about whether the ball should be played forward to the striker. The main priority is to create dangerous situations in front of the opposing team's goal. Each opportunity of bringing the striker into a scoring position must be grasped, even if this involves an element of opportunism. There are a number of situations in which the ball can be played to the striker.

- After a good run
- After regaining possession from the opposing team
- When the opposing team leaves space

"A tall striker, used as a target man, can suddenly speed up the play enormously."

Willy Reynders

The withdrawn striker – a supporting or overlapping role

In most cases, the withdrawn striker functions more like a midfielder, and in youth soccer this is not a good thing. During his development process the number 10 must play an attacking role. He must therefore function more as second striker. Besides supporting the attackers, he must play an overlapping role. He must use every opportunity he has to get forward into and exploit the space between the striker and the opposing team's goal.

15 to 18-year-olds: The details of how the striker and withdrawn striker play depend on the strengths and weaknesses of their own and the opposing team. If the opposing team is weak, the withdrawn striker can play closer to the striker. In this, the oldest, age group, attackers have clear tasks to fulfill. However, they must still have sufficient freedom of movement to develop their own individuality.

10 to 14 year-olds: A too literal application of the above distribution of roles is not wise at this age. A striker who only serves as a target player will not be able to develop fully. 10 and 11-year-olds must be given a lot of space to run with the ball and experiment.

Creating space in the attacking zone

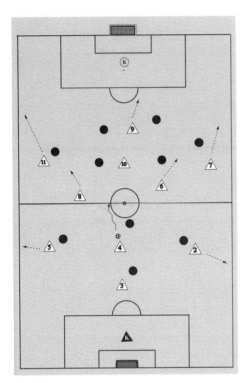

Playing from outside to inside and from inside to outside

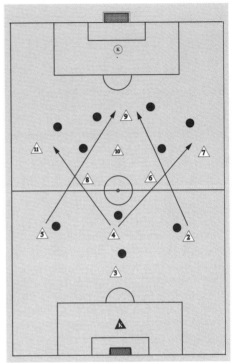

One of the main aims when in possession is to create space. The striker plays a key role here. He must make the playing area as large as possible and play as far forward as possible. In this way he creates space for the other players and is closer to the opposing goal.

15 to 18-year-olds: At this age the creation of space is also dependent on how the opposing team plays. The team in possession will have to take a different approach to creating space against a defensively minded opponent than against one that prefers to play in the opposition's half.

10 to 14 year-olds: The creation of space is one of the basic principles for the younger players. The coach can devote a lot of attention to this.

A key element of the build-up play and the creation of a chance is the diagonal pass:
- **Pass from inside to outside**
From the midfielders/defenders to the wingers/full backs
- **Pass from outside to inside**
From the full backs to the striker/withdrawn striker/midfielders

The pass from outside to outside (from the full backs to the wingers) should be avoided. Such passes are easy to defend against, both individually and collectively. A pass through the center is also only possible in certain circumstances.

15 to 18-year-olds: The players must be aware of this basic rule.

10 to 14 year-olds: The players must be given more freedom to experiment. Tips from the coach can encourage them to play fewer balls from outside to outside.

Creating chances from the team's own half

Example

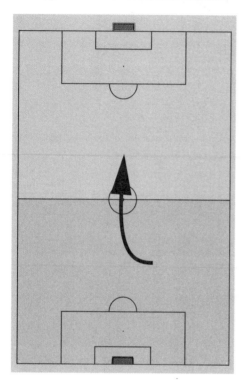

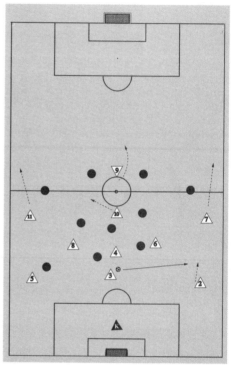

The followings considerations apply in the team's own half:

- Everything has to be done to bridge the distance to the opposing team's half.
- The striker and withdrawn striker must not waste too much energy. Making runs too early or making too many runs reduces their effectiveness.
- The striker must ensure that he remains a threat and keeps the opposing defense under pressure. He must avoid making runs that take him too far back toward his own half.

First of all the playing area must be made as large as possible. The wingers (7 and 11) position themselves as far forward as possible. The striker takes up a position behind the central defenders. This means that he is offside. The opposing defenders have 2 options:

Remain on the same level as the striker

Defenders are used to being able to see attackers. The fact that the striker is behind them makes them uncomfortable.

Drop back

This creates more space for the attacking build-up. The striker often again takes up a position behind the defenders after they drop back. The defenders are therefore confronted with the same problem again.

The striker (9) must then choose the right moment to move into a position to receive the ball. He comes back onside when he can take up a position in which he can receive the ball and the line between him and the ball carrier is free. A good moment to run toward the ball is when it is passed to the right or left back (2 or 5). The withdrawn striker (10) tries to avoid blocking the line between the striker and the ball carrier and takes up a position on the other flank.

The midfielders (6 and 8) play an important supporting role in getting the ball to the striker.

The book "Build-up play" deals with the build-up from the back in detail.

15 to 18-year-olds: The individual players have a greater action radius and this can have a positive influence on the transition from the one half to the other. The players must be aware of the benefits of this. They must also take account of the style of play of the opposing team.

10 to 14 year-olds: The coach can give the players tips about how to build up the play from the one half to the other. The build-up is the main priority. The coach must never discourage the players from showing initiative when they have the ball.

Passing to the feet of the striker or withdrawn striker

Passing to the feet of the attackers can be split up into 4 phases:

- Running into space
- Calling for the ball
- Passing the ball
- Receiving the ball

In the following pages I describe a number of options for each of these phases. There is no such thing as the "correct" way to run into space and call for the ball. The player's characteristics dictate which way he can best do this.

Look at the characteristics of the player before you coach him on how he can best run into space and take up positions in which he is available to receive the ball. Base your coaching on the player's characteristics!

Running into space

Checking away and pushing off from the marker

The attacker gets close to the defender, checks away and then pushes off from him. This way of creating space is usually used by the striker. By getting close to the defender it is easier to determine exactly where he is. A striker is often closely marked. Getting close to the defender helps the attacker to react more quickly and screen the ball. Dynamic players, who can turn quickly, often use this technique to get into positions to receive the ball.

Tips:

- The decision to check away or not depends on the situation. If the attacker is free, checking away is pointless.
- Stand with your knees slightly bent.
- Push yourself off from your opponent.
- Look over your shoulder before you receive the ball.

Coming from behind the defender

Option 1:
The attacker can take up a position behind the defender. The makes it more difficult for the defender to position himself correctly. The attacker can check away diagonally and when the defender tries to get into a new position (behind the attacker) the attacker can run to meet the ball (photo 1). Given the greater freedom of movement, this way of running into space is perfectly suited to the way the withdrawn attacker plays.

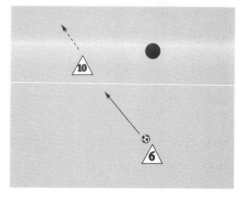

Option 2:
The withdrawn attacker (10) tries to get out of the field of vision of the defender. When the defender looks toward the ball, the attacker calls for the ball. The moment that the defender loses sight of the withdrawn striker, the withdrawn striker puts a few yards between himself and the defender. He can therefore receive the ball in space (photo 1).

If the defender gets too far forward so that he can closely mark the withdrawn striker, the withdrawn striker can run into a position behind him. If the withdrawn striker repeats this run a few times, the defender will not be so keen to get forward. The withdrawn striker will then have more space to receive a pass to his feet (photo 2).

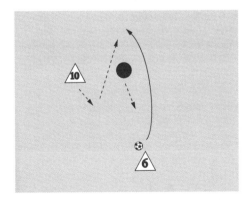

Using the body

Big, strong strikers often make use of this method of making themselves available to receive the ball. The striker uses his body to screen the ball. He 'leans' on the defender and uses his arms to 'feel' exactly where the defender is. Some strikers use their body to turn round the defender.

Tips:
- Use both hands to feel where the defender is.
- Lean against the defender

Coming back from an offside position

Some attackers move into the gap between defenders and goalkeeper and then move back onside. This can make defenders nervous. If the defenders fall back, there is more space between the lines and the distance from the goal is shorter. Leaving the attacker demands good cooperation between the defenders.

Getting into position to receive the ball

The attacker must get into the best position to receive the ball. He must keep as many options open as possible for creating a scoring chance. How, where and when he does this are all important.

Examples:

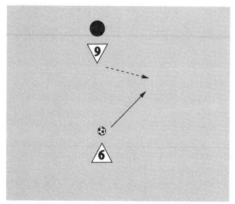

Diagonal run into the path of the ball

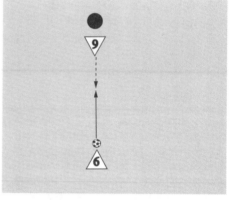

Straight run toward the ball

Diagonal run into the path of the ball

The attacker makes a diagonal run into the path of the ball. The defender has to make a choice. He can follow the attacker, therefore leaving space behind him for the opposing team to exploit, or he can stay where he is, therefore allowing the attacker to receive the ball and turn with it. The defender is then confronted with a frontal 1v1 situation.

Straight run toward the ball

The situation when an attacker runs straight toward the ball is easier to defend against. The attacker has several options in this situation:
- He can turn away from the defender with his first touch.
- He can receive the ball, fake and then turn away.
- He can suddenly sprint toward the ball, gaining a few yards on his marker, and turn as he receives the ball.

Often the striker or withdrawn striker can only lay the ball off or hold it for just a moment. The element of surprise is usually missing.

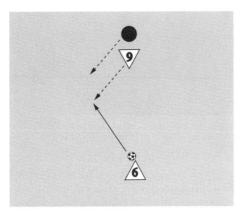

Drawing the defender

Drawing the defender

The attacker can call for the ball at a certain angle. The defender then has to adjust his position and follow the attacker. The moment the defender gets close to the attacker, the attacker can suddenly turn away from him. The attacker must have good technical skills and the ability to turn quickly.

The importance of timing
Given that the situation is always changing, it is difficult to identify the best moment for a player to make himself available. Only at the moment when the player who will pass the ball first receives it is the situation easier to grasp. Good timing is often a question of the players having a good mutual understanding, training together frequently, and perhaps practicing certain routines.

Some tips:
- A lot of players go toward the ball too soon. The trick is to wait until the last possible moment to make your move.
- Eye contact between the passer and the receiver is very important.
- Check away and then back toward the ball at the moment when your teammate receives the ball.

The pass

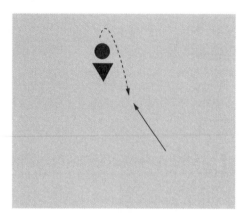

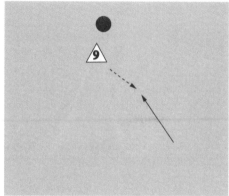

The attacker is closely marked. The best way for him to gain a yard of space is to check away suddenly.

In principle we try to pass the ball as far forward as possible. We try to play the ball to the attacker as often as possible. Depending on the position of the defender, the ball can be played long or short or to the attacker's feet. Correct coaching is essential.

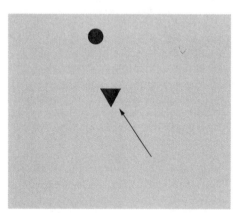

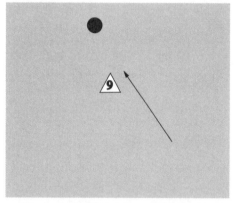

The attacker is not closely marked. He does not need to run toward the ball or check away to create space.

A midfielder must be aware of the technical abilities of the attackers. A pass to an attacker with limited technical ability must be played differently than a pass to a more skillful attacker.

Passing options:

The following ways of passing to an attacker are available:

Pass along the ground
If the situation permits, this is the preferred option, as the attacker is immediately able to continue the move.

Firm, low pass
This has the following advantages:

- The pass reaches its destination faster.
- The pass is often more difficult to defend against. It is more difficult for the defender to get in front of the attacker.

There are also disadvantages:

- A higher level of skill is needed to control the pass when it arrives.
- Because a higher level of skill is required, there is a greater chance that the flow of play will be slowed down or interrupted.

Arcing pass

An arcing pass can be made if there is no way of passing the ball directly to the attacker. There must be sufficient space for the ball to drop in front of the attacker.

Passing tips:

- Eye contact with the attacker is important.
- Communicate with the attacker
- Try to make the pass as easy as possible for the attacker to control. A pass that bounces just in front of a closely marked attacker is often very difficult to control.

"The pass should tell the attacker what he has to do!"

Jos Daerden

Communicating with the ball

Communicating with the ball means passing the ball in such a way that, in effect, the passer tells the receiver what to do next.

Example:

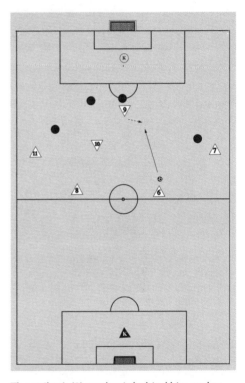

The striker's (9) marker is behind him and to his right. The midfielder (6) plays the ball to the striker's left, away from the defender. The defender cannot intercept the ball and the attacker knows that there is space on his left.

Pace of the pass

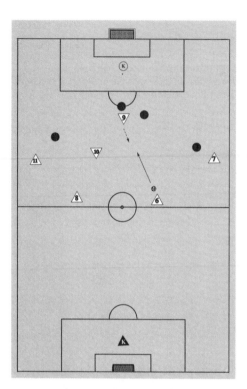 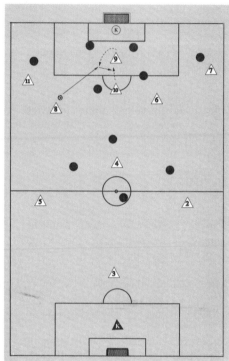

The striker (9) is closely marked. The right midfielder (6) plays a low pass. The striker drops back towards the ball, away from the defenders. This gives him more time and space to receive the ball and continue the move.

The pass must be played directly toward a player who is running to meet it. If it is played to one side, so that he has to run at an angle to the path of the ball, he often has fewer options for dealing with the ball.

There is often very little space in and around the penalty area. The ball must be played at pace to reduce the chance that a defender will intercept it. The left midfielder (8) plays the ball in firmly to the striker (9), who has made himself available. The withdrawn striker (10) joins in and tries to set up a fast combination play or run. Playing a firm pass at pace is often very effective when a player is stationary. If the striker is in motion, the pace of the ball must be reduced.

Receiving the ball
Receiving the ball with the inside of the foot

An attacker who receives the ball with the inside of the foot can easily turn away from his marker or lay the ball off. The ball is more or less shielded by his leg.

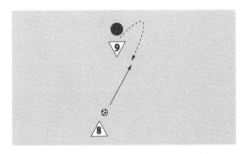

Receiving the ball with the outside of the foot

This is useful when the attacker wants to turn away suddenly and quickly from his marker. The disadvantage is that the ball is not shielded.

Screening the ball with the body and receiving the ball with the outside of the foot

In this case the attacker screens the ball completely. The only disadvantage is that he cannot lay the ball back as efficiently.

Tips:
- Keep running as you receive the ball, so that the defender has no chance of winning the ball.
- The ball should be received in such a way that the direction of the continuation is clear. The ball should not have to be received under the body.
- The ball should be controlled with as few touches as possible.
- Receive the ball in such a way that it can be played immediately.
- A fake can give you more time to receive the ball.

"The way the ball is passed determines how it should be received."

Hein Vanhazebrouck

"A striker who usually lays the ball back can sometimes surprise his marker by turning away with the ball."

Willy Reynders

Laying the ball off

Tips:
Before you lay the ball off
- Ensure that you are well balanced, so the ball will not jump into the air.
- Keep your center of gravity low.

Laying the ball off
- Using the outside foot to lay the ball off sends the ball in a straighter line. This is easier to handle than a spinning ball.
- Lay the ball off diagonally; ensure that it can be played immediately.
- If the ball is traveling at pace, cushion the lay-off by drawing your foot back as you receive the ball.
- Be aware of the position of the defender when you lay the ball off.

"A striker must know when to take the pace off the ball. Holding the ball for a moment instead of laying it off immediately can make the difference between retaining and losing possession."

Jos Daerden

Passing to the feet of the striker or shadow striker

Examples:

Playing the ball from the flank to the feet of the striker (9)

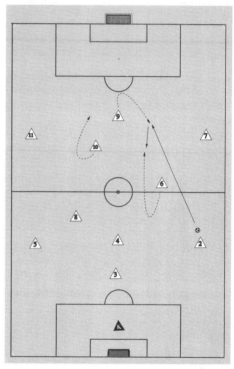

Option 1: With overlap by the withdrawn striker

The right back (2) has the ball. The right midfielder (6) falls back to create more space for the striker (9). The withdrawn striker (10) drops back slightly and leaves the line to the striker free. The striker checks away from the ball and then back toward it. The withdrawn striker exploits the space that has been created and makes a run behind the backs of the central defenders. When the ball is played to the striker, the right midfielder (6) joins in too. This option is preferable because the withdrawn striker poses a threat in front of the goal.

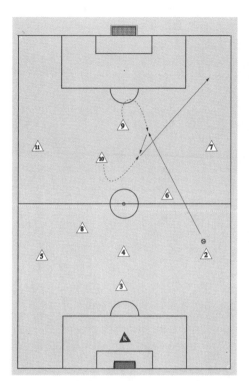

Option 2: With the withdrawn striker playing a supporting role

Playing the ball from the flank to the feet of the withdrawn striker (10)

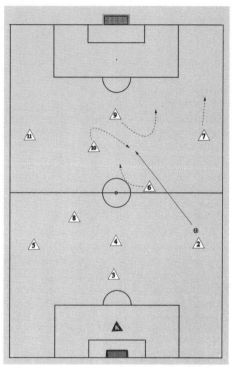

In this situation the withdrawn striker (10) provides support. The forward runs from behind the striker (9) can be made by midfielders (6 or 8). In some cases, however, the distance will be too great to create any danger in front of the goal.

The withdrawn striker has a supporting role in this situation. When the striker lays the ball off, he can pass immediately to one of the wingers (7 or 11).

When the ball is played forward to the central attackers, it should preferably be passed to the striker (9), as he is closest to the goal and offers more options. When the striker is difficult to reach, the withdrawn striker can move forward to act as a second advanced striker. After the striker has made himself available, he should move back into the center again, leaving space for the withdrawn striker to make himself available.

Example:
The right back (2) has the ball. The right midfielder (6) drops back to create space for the withdrawn striker (10). The striker (9) comes toward the ball, but cannot be reached. He returns to his central position. The withdrawn striker runs into the space left by the striker. The withdrawn striker can hold the ball, lay it off or make a run with it.

Variation on passing to feet

Passing to feet through the center

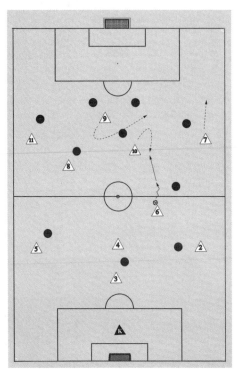

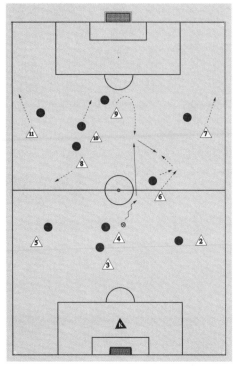

The withdrawn striker (10) checks away diagonally forward and then checks back toward the ball. The striker (9) checks away diagonally and then checks back behind the back of the withdrawn striker. This run creates confusion in the mind of the defender marking the withdrawn striker. If he does not follow the withdrawn striker, the ball can be played to the withdrawn striker, who can then turn with it. He might then be able to play a 1-2 with the striker, who has again made himself available.

It is often, but not always, impossible to pass the ball forward down the center. If it can be played, such a pass is very effective.

The central midfielder (4) has the ball. The two midfielders create space by making diagonal runs away from him. Opponent (a) follows, leaving space for a forward pass to the striker (9). The midfielders then move up to support him. The effectiveness of the forward pass depends on the passing skills of the central defender (4).

> "You can win games by using your brain. If you observe your opponent at the start of the game, you can learn a lot. How mobile is he? Is he fast over the first few yards? Which is his weaker foot?"
>
> *Dirk Kuyt, striker, Feyenoord Rotterdam*

Playing an arcing pass

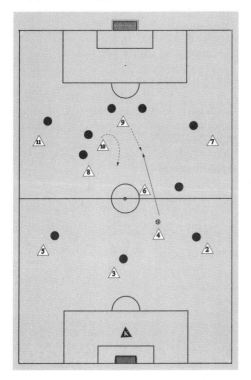 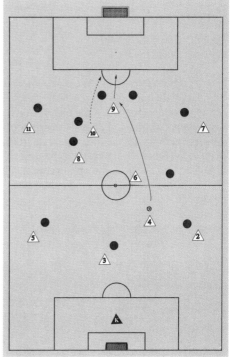

Option 1:
The withdrawn striker (10) gets close to his opponent and draws him in the direction of the ball. This creates space for the striker (9) to receive the arcing ball. At the moment when the pass is played, the withdrawn striker moves to support the striker. Playing an arcing pass is a good option when the opposing team is defending a long way from its goal and pressuring the ball.

Option 2:
In this situation the pass is more opportunistic. The ball is played forward to the striker (9). The withdrawn striker or another player makes a run behind the striker and tries to win the win the ball when the striker heads it on.

Forward pass to the striker or the withdrawn striker

There are two ways of playing the pass:
Option 1: Down the center
Option 2: Down the flank

The pass down the center has the advantage that the player immediately appears in front of and threatens the goal. If the ball is passed to the flank, a number of phases have to be gone through before the ball appears in front of the goal. There is therefore less chance of threatening the goal. The option chosen also depends on the passer's technique and insight.

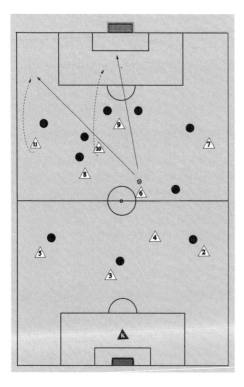

Forward pass to the striker (9) and the withdrawn striker (10)

This can be divided into three phases:
   - Running into space
   - Passing the ball
   - Receiving the ball

A number of possibilities are described below. How they are used depends on the abilities of the players.

Running into space

From a standing start

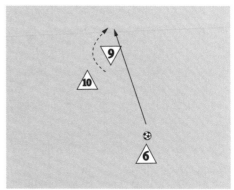

A player who makes a sudden forward run from a standing start can surprise the opposition. This unexpected way of running into space demands specific abilities from the attacker (a fast start, insight, etc.) and from the passer. An attacker who makes a number of forward runs from a standing start can create confusion in the opposing defense. The defenders may mark less closely.

Patrick Kluivert sprints forward from a standing start. This can catch out a defender who expects him always to check away first.

Drawing an opponent and making a run behind his back

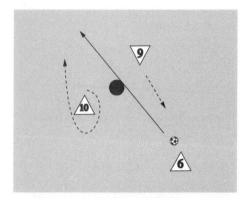

The withdrawn striker gets close to his marker and tries to draw him toward the ball. If the defender follows him, the striker makes a run into the space left by the defender. The withdrawn striker must stand at an angle to the defender (see photo). This gives him an advantage when he makes a forward run, as the defender must turn to follow him.

Getting out of the defender's field of view

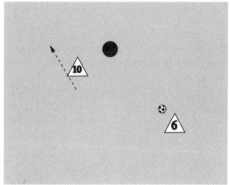

Diagram 1

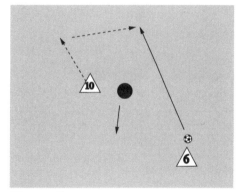

Diagram 2

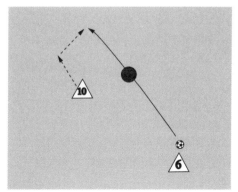

Diagram 3

The withdrawn striker moves diagonally until
he is standing outside the field of vision of the
defender (diagram 1). The withdrawn striker
acts as though he wants the ball played to
his feet. The defender expects this and moves
to cover the line of the pass. The withdrawn
striker then makes a run across and behind
the defender (diagram 2). In some cases the
withdrawn striker may run further forward
(diagram 3).

Running wide

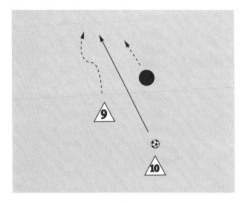

The attacker makes a forward run away from
the ball and is shadowed by a defender. At
the last moment the attacker swerves wide
to make space for a pass. Sometimes running
wide can be a good way to avoid running into
an offside position.

Blocking the defender on the other side

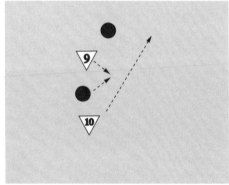

When the withdrawn striker (10) makes a
forward run, the striker (9) can block the withdrawn striker's marker, so that the withdrawn
striker has more space in which to receive the
ball.

Tips:

- Keep the space free; do not go forward too
  soon
  - Check away to the side first and then make
    the forward run (avoid running into an
    offside position)
- Stay in eye contact with the ball carrier as
  you run
- Run with full conviction

Passing

The most effective moment to pass to players in advanced positions is:
- after wining the ball
- after a fast combination play
- in a fast counterattack

Playing the ball forward down the center

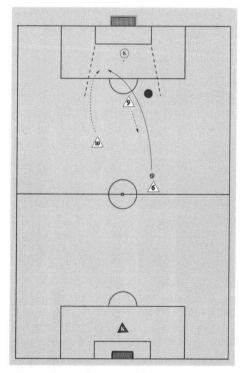

The ball must be passed as effectively as possible, taking account of the position of the defender and the goalkeeper. The attacker making the forward run must receive the ball as close to goal as possible. An attacker who moves out toward the flanks too often is less of a threat in front of goal.

Passing the ball forward to the flank

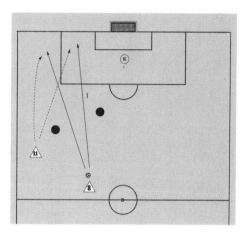

A forward pass to a winger is often aimed into the corner of the field. This means that the winger has to make a long and difficult cross. It is important that a winger receives a forward pass as close to the goal as possible. In this situation it is better for the midfielder to play the ball inside (line 1). The distance from the goal is shorter and the pass is more difficult for the defenders to intercept.

Tips:

Before passing the ball
- Eye contact with the attacker

The pass
- Play a fast firm pass; not too high.
- Do not slow down the attack – pass the ball in front of the winger.
- Try to adapt your technique to the space and the positions of the defenders.
  - Plenty of space technique = Fast pass or long forward ball that holds up
  - Tight space technique = Fast short pass or ball that holds up.

Receiving the ball

Cutting across the opposing player

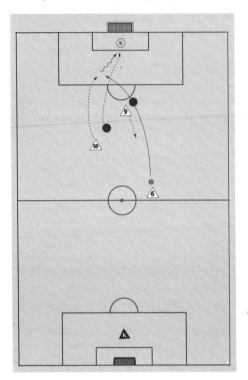

Taking up central positions near the goal

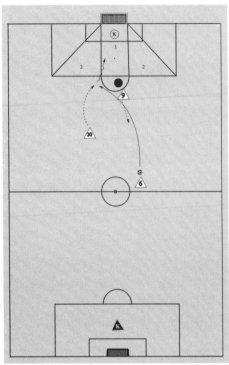

After receiving the ball, it is important top keep the opposing player at a distance. One way of doing this is to cut across his path.

When an attacker receives the ball, he should be as central as possible in front of the goal (zone 1). An attacker who moves away from this zone too often (zone 2 or 3) is often at too acute an angle to the goal and is therefore less dangerous.

"Gordon Strachan, the coach of Coventry, broadened my skills as an attacker. He taught me how to breach a defense and how to choose the right moment to appear in the penalty area. I am convinced that a coach cannot make a player, but he can point you in the right direction."

Cedric Roussel, striker, Racing Genk

Tips:
- Keep the tempo high.
- Do not slow the pace of the move down as you receive the ball.
- Take the ball on your foot, chest, etc.
- Try to use your outside foot to take the ball.
- If no opponent is close to you and you have a lot of ground to cover, you can push the ball forward and run with it.

Long forward pass to striker or withdrawn striker

Examples:

Long forward pass to striker from the flank

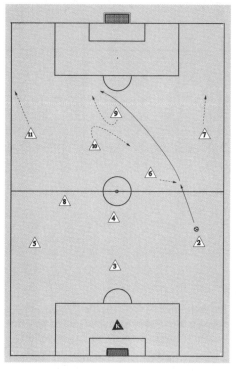

Forward pass to the withdrawn striker from the flank

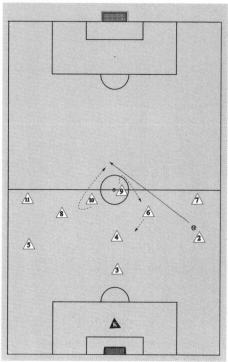

The withdrawn striker (10) comes toward the ball and the striker (9) makes a forward run. The ball must reach the striker quickly. The midfielder (6) must pass the ball forward in the blink of an eye.

The striker first makes a diagonal run away from the ball. This creates space for him to receive the ball. The easiest way to control the ball is using his chest or the outside foot.

The right back (2) has the ball. The striker (9) makes a run toward the ball, creating space for the withdrawn striker (10). The withdrawn striker moves outside the field of view of his marker and then runs into the space behind the striker. The withdrawn striker must react quickly to exploit the space created by the striker. The distance between the striker and withdrawn striker must not be too large. The chance of success in this situation is greatest when there is a lot of space behind the defenders.

> "Most players run toward the ball. However, runs away from the ball are more likely to surprise the opposition."
>
> *Ariël Jacobs*

41

Forward pass down the center to the withdrawn striker

Variation of the forward pass

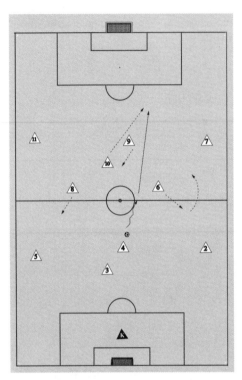

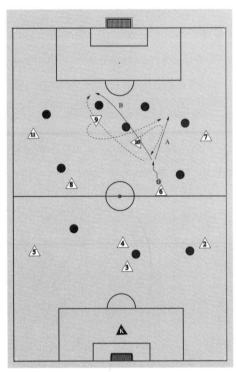

This situation arises when the opposition unexpectedly loses possession or when a fast counterattack is staged. The striker (9) creates space for the withdrawn striker (10) to run into. The defensive midfielder (4) wins the ball and immediately passes it forward down the center.

The withdrawn striker (10) checks away diagonally and makes a run toward the ball. The striker (9) checks away diagonally and then runs into the space behind the withdrawn striker. The opposing player marking the withdrawn striker now has a problem. If he does not follow the withdrawn striker, the shadow striker can receive the ball and turn with it and possibly play a 1-2 with the striker. If he does follow the withdrawn striker, the ball can be played to the striker (line A). If the striker cannot be reached, the withdrawn striker can make a forward run behind the defenders to receive the ball (line B).

The tasks of the midfielders

The complexity of the midfield

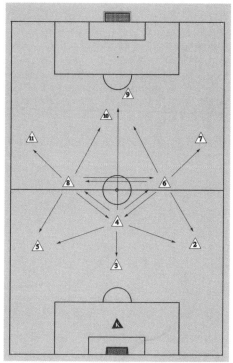

The midfield positions are the most difficult on the field. In view of their central positions, midfielders have to develop a lot of insight. A midfielder must learn positional play relative to the players in front of him (attackers), players outside of him (full backs and wingers) and players behind him (defenders). They have to be aware of everything happening in the 360 degrees around them! This makes life difficult. In view of the positional requirements on midfielders, coaching in build-up play is essential. The coach must stimulate the midfielders and give them a framework that encourages them without submerging their own individuality.

"Many midfielders play the ball square because they prefer to stay away from crowded situations. That is the simplest solution. Really they should show their quality by seeking crowded situations and creating space by taking the ball past an opponent."

Gerald Vanenburg

Individual requirements on midfielders

- The main objective is to create dangerous situations in front of the opposing team's goal.
- They must be able to take up good positions relative to the opposing players and the ball. Through their positional play, they create more options when in possession.
- They must make one-touch passes as often as possible.
- They must have a good ball control to allow them to create more passing options.
- They must be able to communicate through their passes.
- Midfielders must be able to think one or two steps ahead.
- Midfielders must be able to maintain good positional balance relative to each other.
- Midfielders must be able to maintain a good balance between the numbers of players in front of and behind the ball.

Collective requirements on midfielders

Facilitate build-up play by:

- Creating space to enable the ball to be passed wide and forward.
- Supporting defenders, attackers and each other.
- Switching the play to the other flank.
- Making runs off the ball.
- Making runs with the ball.

The midfielder's infiltration role

Midfielders have an important supporting function with regard to the attackers. They can also be a key weapon in infiltrating the defensive line of the opposing team. Midfielders who make forward runs can provide the necessary variation in the penalty area. The opposing team often has difficulty dealing with such runs by midfielders.

> "If you want to win the league, you have to score 75 to 100 goals. The attackers will score about 45. That leaves 30 to 35. Some of these will be scored from restart plays such as free kicks and corners. The others have to come from open play. Midfielders who can score goals are therefore very important."
>
> *Aimé Antheunis*

Examples:

Support function

Creating space for a forward pass to the striker and making a forward run in support

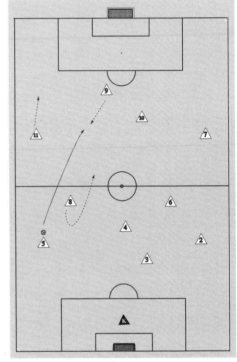

The left midfielder (8) drops back and thus creates space for a forward pass. After the left back (5) passes to the striker (9), the left midfielder makes a forward run to support him.

Ideally, the players will anticipate the situation faster than the opposition. When the pass is on its way, the player must already be making his forward run. If the midfielder joins in early, the chance of a good continuation of the move is greater, and even if the striker loses possession, the midfielder is in a good position relative to his direct opponent.

> *The pace of the move depends on the players behind the ball.*

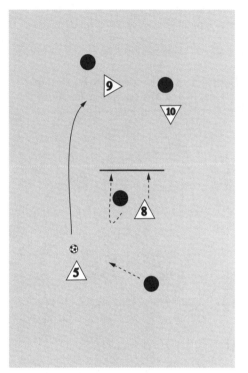 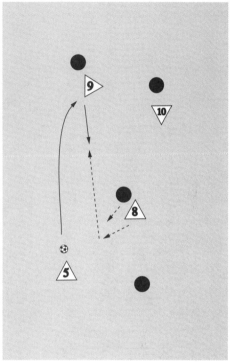

In this situation, the left midfielder (8) fails to anticipate the move early enough. His opponent is therefore able to stay level with him.

The left midfielder (8) draws his marker with him toward the ball. At the moment when the ball is played, he makes a forward run in support. He therefore creates a numerical advantage relative to his marker.

"Some players set off too late but still win the duel with their opponent. This is still poor support play, in my opinion, because you can avoid the duel by anticipating the move more quickly."

Jan Olde Riekerink

45

Infiltration function

Infiltration by the right or left midfielder (6 or 8)

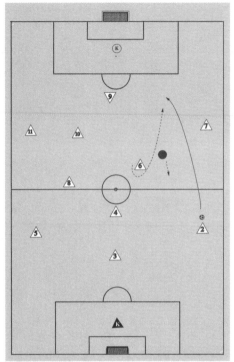

The right midfielder (6) draws his marker with him toward the ball, then makes a forward run behind his marker's back. If the full back cannot immediately play a forward pass, the midfielder's run may create other opportunities:

- If the defender marking the striker (9) moves across to cover the midfielder's run, the striker has space to make a run toward the ball.
- If the run is unsuccessful, the left midfielder (8) can make a forward run.

If one midfielder makes a forward run, the other midfielder must cover the space in case the opposition gains possession.

Withdrawn striker and right and left midfielder (6 and 8) interchange positions

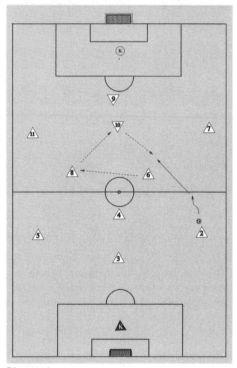

Diagram 1

The midfielders (6 and 8) and the withdrawn striker (10) interchange positions (diagram 1).
- The withdrawn striker runs toward the ball and arrives at the position of the right midfielder (6).
- The left midfielder (8) makes a forward run and takes over the position of the withdrawn striker.
- The right midfielder takes over the position of the left midfielder.

The purpose of these positional interchanges is to make it more difficult for the opposition to keep track of the withdrawn striker and the midfielders. The positional switches can also involve just 2 players – in the example the right midfielder (6) makes a forward run and the withdrawn striker (10) makes a run toward the ball (see diagram 2).

Passing to the third man

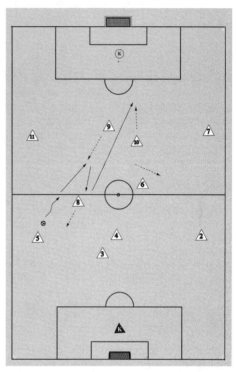

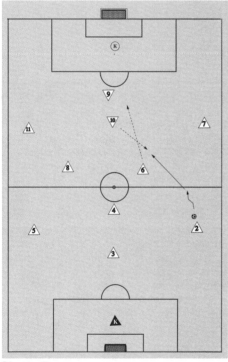

Diagram 2

Combination plays between three players can be used to create chances. Defenders often follow only the player who passes the ball and the player who receives it. The third player is often not involved in the play and therefore has a little more time and space. This is especially so if he makes his move from midfield. The third player often injects pace into a play. The third man can make a forward run or move closer to the other two to help set up a fast combination.

In many cases the third man positions himself on the same side of field as the ball. Involving a third man who is out of the field of view of the opposing player can create the most danger.

Make use of the space between the lines

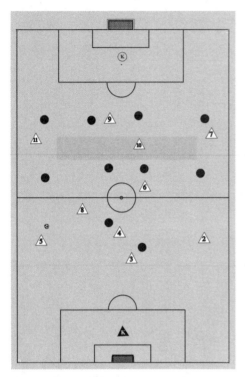

A lot of teams opt for zonal marking. The players take up positions relative to the ball. As a result they form "positioned lines." If an attacker positions himself in the space between two lines, the opposing players may not be sure who is responsible for covering him.

Drawing an opponent away when the ball is played in from the flank

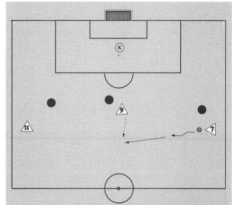

The right winger (7) runs infield with the ball. The striker (9) stands next to his marker and checks away diagonally from him at the very last moment. This creates a frontal 1 v 1 situation.

"When you play between the lines, you don't just have to know where the opposition players are positioned, you must also know where your teammates are."

Mark Degryse

Coaching:
Play	Play the ball
Free	No opponent close to you
Lay off	Lay the ball off to the right winger
Hold	Hold the ball
Back	Play the ball back

Tactical choices

Between two central defenders and two midfielders

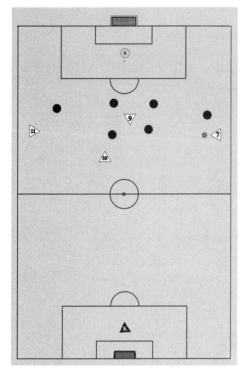

Some opponents play with four defenders and two midfielders. The striker (9) and the withdrawn striker (10) have very little space.

Option 1:

The striker must play between the opposition's lines and try to cause confusion between the defenders and midfielders. He does this by moving alternately forward (into the defenders' zone) and back (into the midfielders' zone). As a result he may gain a fraction more time to receive a pass and turn with the ball, etc.

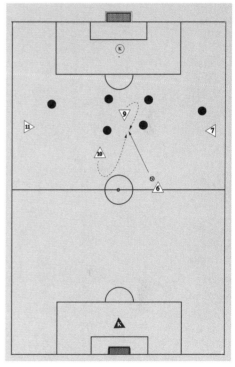

"If a real defender marked me, the coach asked me to draw him back into the midfield zone. If a midfielder marked me, I was to draw him forward into the defensive zone. Midfielders don't like to play in the defense."

Dennis Bergkamp on Louis van Gaal

Option 2:
The withdrawn striker (10) plays further forward and tries to draw one of the central defenders away from the center, thus creating more space for the striker (9). In this situation the distance between the striker and the withdrawn striker can be greater than usual. The two central defenders therefore cannot mark the two attackers so easily.

Option 3:
The withdrawn striker falls back and plays more between the right and left midfielders (6 and 8). The two central defenders are therefore forced to play more out of their zone and the striker has more space.

Playing deep

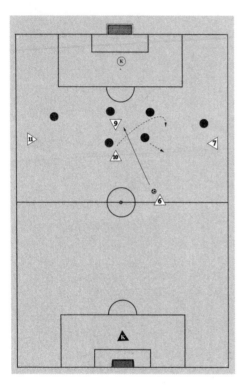

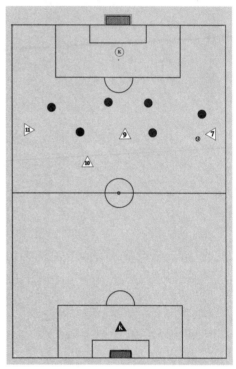

Most strikers play in the zone covered by the central defenders. The defenders can therefore often neutralize them more easily. The defenders' task is more difficult if the striker plays deeper. The distribution of tasks between the opposing players is less clear (who marks whom?). Defenders are often used to marking an attacker and have problems playing when they have no direct opponent. This tactic creates infiltration opportunities for other players.

Playing against a defensive midfielder

More variation in the run lines

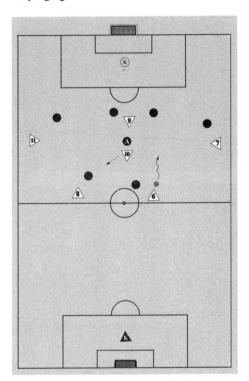

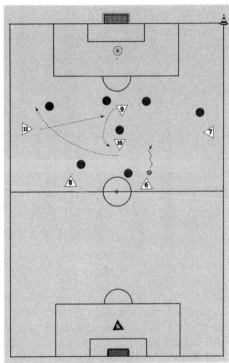

In this situation, the objective is for the withdrawn striker (10) to draw the defensive midfielder (A) out of his zone. The withdrawn striker gets close to the defensive midfielder, who is therefore responsible for marking him, and then checks away diagonally. The defensive midfielder faces a dilemma. If he follows the withdrawn striker he will leave space for the striker. If he does not follow, the withdrawn striker will be available to receive the ball.

In this situation the left winger (11), the withdrawn striker (10) and the striker (9) interchange positions. This can create chaos in the opposing team and is less easy to defend against. The disadvantage of this tactic is that it may weaken the team's organization when it loses possession.

Coaching ball skills

Besides the aims of the game, we also devote attention to the individual technique of young soccer players. I am convinced that the coaching of ball skills has a place in youth soccer. The coaching of the skills needed to deceive an opponent and dribble past him brings added value to the learning process of young soccer players.

I view the coaching of ball skills more as fundamental support. Most of the practice sessions will be devoted to match-related drills (with the obstacles and constraints encountered in real matches, such as opponents, teammates, time, space and a defined playing area). I base my treatment of technical skills on real matches.

By ball skills we mean changing direction and turning with the ball, faking, etc.

The main objectives of attacking play are to create chances and score goals. Ball skills are subordinate to these objectives. Technique is the means with which these objectives are realized (by taking the ball past an opponent, playing an attacker into space, etc.).

Attacking play requires more than dribbling tricks and fakes. Technical skill such as turning away from an opponent and getting the ball into space are frequently encountered in these drills.

The technical skills I deal with in the attacking play module are directly related to the aims of the game. I have chosen simple, effective and realistic skills that can help the players to create chances. The most frequently occurring situations in build-up play are:

- Opponent in front
- Opponent behind

The aims of attacking play

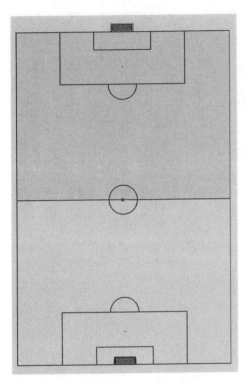

Aims:
- To create danger in the opposing team's penalty area.
- To score goals.

Means:
- Individual runs, combinations, forward passes, shots at goal.
- Crosses.

Conclusion:
Technical ball skills support these aims.

Opponent in front

Inside – outside
The attacker starts a run in the center.

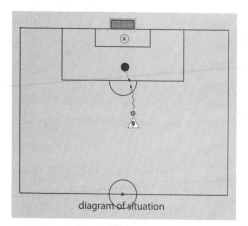

diagram of situation

photo of situation

Tips:
- Fake to go to the left.
- Take a few steps to the left.
- Knees slightly bent.
- Accelerate explosively.

Description of technique
Step 1: Your left leg is your standing leg.
Step 2: Push the ball inside with the inside of your right foot.
Step 3: Immediately push the ball in the other direction with the outside of your right foot.

Inside – stepover – outside

The attacker starts a run in the center.

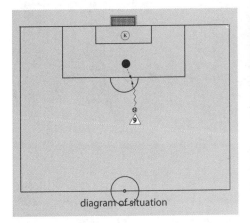

diagram of situation

1

photo of situation

Tip:
- Fake to go to the right.
- Take a few steps to the left.
- Knees slightly bent.
- Accelerate explosively.

2

Description of technique

Step 1: Your left leg is your standing leg.

Step 2: Push the ball inside with the inside of your right foot.

Step 3: Fake to take the ball in the other direction using the outside of the same foot, but step sideways over the ball.

Step 4: Take the ball on with the outside of the other foot.

Double scissor

The attacker starts a run in the center.

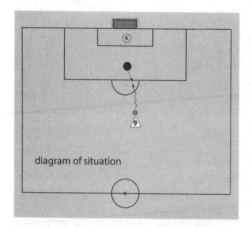

diagram of situation

photo of situation

Tips:
- Fake to go to one side then the other.
- Make the movement as quickly as possible
- Knees slightly bent

Description of technique

Step 1: Place your left foot beside the ball.

Step 2: Make a scissor movement (from the inside to the outside) round the ball with your right foot.

Step 3: Place your right foot beside the ball.

Step 4: Make a scissor movement (from the inside to the outside) round the ball with your left foot.

Step 5: Take the ball on with the outside of the right foot.

Stepover inside

The attacker starts a run in the center.

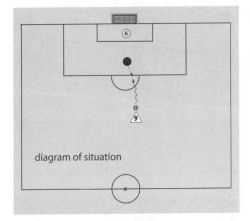

diagram of situation

photo of situation

Tips:
- Fake to go to one side then the other.
- Make the movement as quickly as possible
- Knees slightly bent
- Accelerate explosively.

Description of technique

Step 1: Step over the ball with your right foot (from outside to inside).

Step 2: Take the ball on immediately with the outside of the same foot.

Scissor inside

The attacker starts a run in the center.

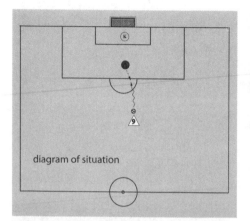

diagram of situation

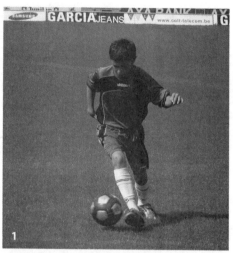

photo of situation

Tips:
- Fake to go to inside.
- Make the movement as quickly as possible
- Knees slightly bent
- Accelerate explosively.

Description of technique

Step 1: Make a scissor movement (from the inside to the outside) round the ball with your right foot.

Step 2: Take the ball toward the outside immediately with the outside of the right foot.

Scissor inside

The attacker starts a run in the center.

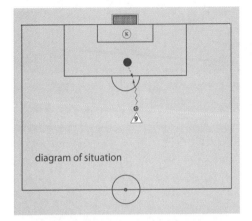

diagram of situation

photo of situation

Tips:
- This movement is ideal for making an inside run.
- Make the movement as quickly as possible
- Knees slightly bent
- Accelerate explosively.

Description of technique
Step 1: Step over the ball with your right foot (from inside to outside).
Step 2: Take the ball toward the inside immediately with the inside of the same foot.

Stepover outside and intermediate step

The attacker starts a run in the center.

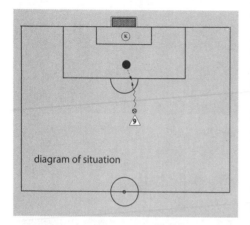

diagram of situation

1

2

photo of situation

3

Tips:
- Use your body; fake to go past your opponent on the left.
- Knees slightly bent.
- Make the movement as quickly as possible.
- Knees slightly bent.
- Accelerate explosively.

Description of technique

Step 1: Place your left foot beside the ball.

Step 2: Step over the ball with your right foot (from inside to outside).

Step 3: Take an intermediate step (fake) with your left foot.

Step 4: Take the ball on with the outside of the right foot.

Drag inside

The attacker starts a run in the center.

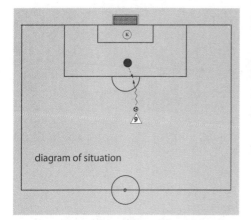

diagram of situation

photo of situation

Tips:
- This movement is ideal for making an inside run.
- Lean to the left.
- If your opponent blocks your path inside, you can take the ball to the outside with the outside of your right foot.
- Keep your foot in contact with the ball.
- Make the movement as quickly as possible.
- Accelerate explosively.

Description of technique

Step 1: Place your left foot diagonally beside the ball.

Step 2: Drag the ball inside with the inside of the right foot.

Okocha movement

The attacker starts a run in the center.

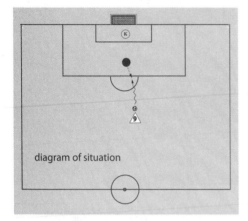

diagram of situation

photo of situation

Tips:
- Fake with your body.
- Step energetically over the ball to the inside.
- Accelerate explosively.

Description of technique

Step 1: Place your left foot beside the ball.

Step 2: Use the sole of your right foot to roll the ball from outside to inside.

Step 3: Step over the ball with your left foot from outside to inside.

Step 4: Take the ball on with the outside of the foot.

Fake to the outside and inside alternately

The attacker starts a run in the center.

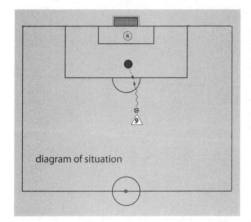

diagram of situation

photo of situation

Tips:
- Do this at speed.
- Fake with your body.
- You can tap the ball outside or inside several times before suddenly taking it in the opposite direction.
- You can combine this movement with stepovers, scissor, etc.
- Try to make your opponent lose his balance.
- Accelerate explosively.

Description of technique

Step 1: Tap the ball inside using the inside of the foot.

Step 2: Tap the ball outside using the outside of the foot.

Opponent behind

I have divided 1v1 situations with an opponent behind the attacker into 3 groups:
- Turning immediately
- Receiving, faking and turning
- Drawing the opponent to one side and then turning away to the other side

Turning immediately

Turning with the outside of the foot
The attacker receives the ball with his back to the goal and turns away from his opponent in one movement.

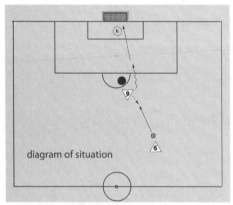

diagram of situation

photo of situation

Description of technique
Step 1: Move your right knee to the outside.
Step 2: Take the ball with the outside of the foot.
Step 3: Shield the ball immediately with the inside of the foot.

Tips:
- Knees slightly bent
- Glance over your shoulder
- Fake to go in one direction before receiving the ball

Turning with the inside of the foot

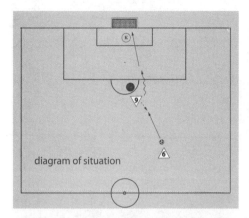

diagram of situation

photo of situation

The attacker receives the ball with his back to the goal and turns away from his opponent in one movement.

Tips:
- Knees slightly bent
- Glance over your shoulder
- Fake to go in one direction before receiving the ball
- Be aware of the position of your opponent. There must enough space in which to turn. If your opponent covers the space well, you might run into him.

Description of technique
Step 1: Take the ball on with the inside of the foot.

Step 3: Shield the ball immediately with the outside of the foot.

Taking the ball behind your standing leg

The attacker receives the ball with his back to the goal and turns away from his opponent in one movement.

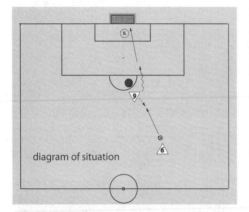

diagram of situation

photo of situation

Tips:
- Glance over your shoulder

Description of technique

Step 1: The midfielder takes a large step, placing his right foot ahead and to the right of the ball, and allows the ball to run between his feet.

Step 2: He then pushes the ball across the back of his right foot, using the inside of his left foot.

Step 3: He turns to his right and runs on with the ball.

Receiving, faking and turning

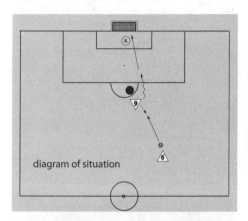

diagram of situation

photo of situation

Stepover and turn away from your opponent

The attacker receives the ball with his back to the goal. He steps over the ball to the left, then turns away with the ball to the right, using the inside of his left foot.

Tips:
You can also use the outside of the foot to turn away.

Description of technique

Step 1: Take the ball to right with your right foot and step over it from outside to inside, using your right foot.

Step 2: Turn away with the ball, using the inside of your left foot.

Making a scissor movement and turning away

The attacker receives the ball with his back to the goal. He makes a scissor movement to the outside and then turns away with the ball using the outside of the other foot.

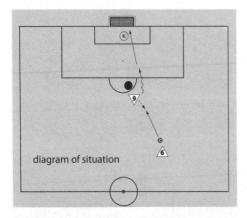

diagram of situation

photo of situation

Description of technique

Step 1: When you receive the ball, make a scissor movement round the ball with your right foot (from inside to out side).

Step 2: Use the outside of your left foot to turn away from your opponent and take the ball on.

Tips:
- Knees slightly bent
- Make the movement as quickly as possible

Letting the ball run through and cutting inside

The attacker receives the ball with his back to the goal. He allows the ball to run through and then cuts it inside to take it past the opposing player.

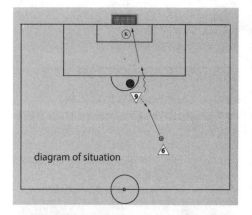

diagram of situation

photo of situation

Description of technique

Step 1: Allow the ball to run through close to your feet.

Step 2: Use the inside of your right foot to cut the ball inside, so that it runs across and past the defender.

Step 3: Shoot with your left foot.

Tips:

- Before cutting the ball inside the attacker can feint to shoot. The defender automatically tends to try to block the shot.

- Cut the ball back firmly across and past the defender.

Drawing an opponent to one side and turning away to the other

Turning back using the outside of the foot
The attacker draws the defender to one side and then turns away in the other direction.

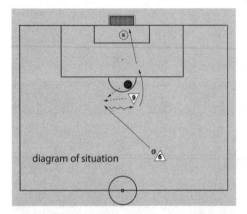

diagram of situation

Description of technique
Step 1: Place your right foot ahead of the ball.
Step 2: Use the outside of your left foot to turn away in the other direction.
Step 3: Shoot with your left foot or run on.

photo of situation

Tips:
- Take as few steps as possible and turn back as soon as possible.
- Turn back explosively

Turning back using the inside of the foot

The attacker draws the defender to one side and then turns away in the other direction.

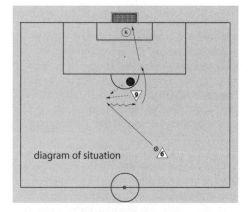

diagram of situation

photo of situation

Description of technique

Step 1: Place your right foot ahead of the ball.

Step 2: Use the inside of your right foot to turn away in the other direction.

Step 3: Shoot with your right foot or run on.

Tips:
- Take as few steps as possible and turn back as soon as possible.
- Turn back explosively

TRAINING FOR 1v1 SITUATIONS WITH AN OPPONENT IN FRONT OR AN OPPONENT BEHIND

In the central attack module, the main focus is 1v1 situations with an opponent in front or an opponent behind. These are the 1v1 situations that occur most frequently in the creation of chances.

There are various ways of coaching for 1v1 situations with an opponent in front or an opponent behind. In practice, all sorts of drills are used to encourage players to dribble past their direct opponent. The chosen drills are not always very effective. In many cases they are not related to real game situations and the trick and fake movements are practiced for their own sake.

Each drill should have a certain return. The objective is to use drills that enable techniques to be applied in real game situations as quickly as possible. The coach has to take a number of factors into consideration. These factors have an influence on the content of the drills.

The objective is to use the movements in real game situations as quickly as possible.

The level of skill of the players
Young soccer players who have already acquired some level of skill will be able to start functional drills or practice drills with opponents sooner.

Age group
In the case of the younger players, more emphasis will be placed on the movements needed to dribble past an opponent. Individual drills will be used. Older groups will mainly carry out drills involving opponents.

Number of training sessions per week
The coach can focus more on the movements if there are 3 sessions per week than if there is only one.

The coach's background
In some cases the coach's background plays a role. A coach who was a skillful right winger will have a different approach to the movements needed to dribble past an opponent than a former defender.

The coach's skills
The coach's level of skill has a major influence on the coaching yield and the translation of ball skills into practice.

It is impossible to lay down a fixed pattern for coaching the application of the movements needed to dribble past an opponent in real games. The practical situation determines the steps to be taken.

Requirements for coaching ball skills and the 1v1 situation

- Ball skills and the 1v1 situation must be aligned to a position or a situation arising from a position.
- The coaching of ball skills must take account of the specific qualities of each individual player.
- Players must be encouraged to think about ball skills while learning how to improve them. Aspects such as "when", "how" and "where" are important.
- The place where the players practice the skill or 1v1 situation must bear a relationship to a real match situation.
- The players must play in the right direction.
- There must be a follow-up to the technical skill.
- The movement must be simple and efficient

I have divided the translation of 1v1 situations into real game situations into 5 steps. It is not the intention that the coach should go through these 5 phases. Depending on the needs of the group, the time available, the age of the players, and the coach's skills and background, the coach can choose from the following steps:

1. **Individual coaching of the movements needed to dribble past an opponent**
2. **Functional coaching of the movements needed to dribble past an opponent**
3. **1v1 with a "handicapped" defender**
4. **1v1**
5. **Translation of 1v1 into a match situation**

Step 1: Individual coaching

In the requirements for coaching ball skills, I mainly refer to functional coaching of the movements needed to dribble past an opponent. In view of the faster yield, these drills are preferred. Individual encouragement of players is an option if there is sufficient coaching time available. The aim of individual drills is to practice the technical and coordinative aspects of ball skills. Since no opponents or match situations are involved, the players are not distracted but can focus completely on the movement. The movement can be repeated dozens of times until it becomes second nature.

The aim is for the player to be able to carry out the movement perfectly. Unnecessary obstacles (complex drills, run lines and situations) must be avoided.

Unfortunately, individual coaching of the movements needed to dribble past an opponent is not always focused on technique alone. The drills are often too complex (difficult run lines and situations) and the techniques are not functional. The players are therefore occupied more with the organization, while the aim of the drill (practicing a technique or movement) fades into the background.

Individual drills must be as simple and realistic as possible. Simple drills with lots of repetition and functional movements take precedence. They are useful aids for learning how to repeat techniques faultlessly time after time. They can best be carried out at the start of a training session. When the coach sees that the players have mastered the techniques, he can switch to more functional drills.

Tips:
- Ensure that the movements are efficient and realistic.
- Carry out the movement step by step. Try to explain the movement in stages.
- Ensure first of all that the movement is carried out properly.
- The speed of execution of the movement can then be increased.
- Practice the movements on both sides of the field.
- Coach combinations of movements.
- Leave the players to themselves at first. Let them get on with it. Observe which players have which skills. Then try to broaden their range of skills.
- Do not try to do too much at once.
- It is fun to link a movement with a player's name, for example the "Peter trick."
- Try to encourage the players to practice movements regularly. The start of the training session (warming up) is the best time.
- Make sure that lots of repetitions are guaranteed.
- Choose simple organizational forms.
- Give the players homework.

"Jan Koller was unable to turn using the inside of the foot. However, he was good at turning by taking the ball behind his standing leg. So we focused on this movement. We opted for functional technique based on the player's inherent skills. Technique must be subordinate to speed of action."

Willy Reynders, who coached the Czech international at Sporting Lokeren a few years ago

75

Example of an individual drill:

With an opponent behind

The players practice the following movements:
- Turning immediately
- Receiving, faking and turning
- Drawing an opponent to one side

With opponent in front

The players practice the following movements:
- Dragging inside
- Inside – outside
- Double scissor

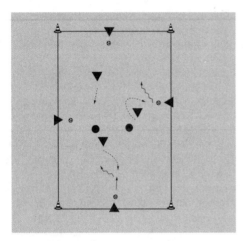

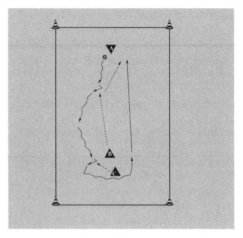

Organization:
- The players run at random in the area and call for the ball from the players on the sidelines.
- Lay-off, call for the ball again, turn away.
- Two defenders are introduced into the area. They can try to win the ball.

Coaching:
See tips for 1v1 situations with a defender behind.

Organization:
- Player A runs with the ball.
- Player B runs to meet player A and takes over his position.
- Player A takes the ball past player B with a fake or dribbling movement.
- Player A takes the ball past player C with a fake or dribbling movement.
- After passing player C he turns back and passes to player B.
- We start again.

Variations:
- Player C defends a line ("handicapped" defender)
- Player C defends a goal (1v1 situation)

Coaching:
See tips for 1v1 situations with a defender behind.

Step 2: Functional coaching of ball skills

Functional coaching of ball skills is clearer for the players. The "recognition factor" is greater. The location on the field, the direction of play and the situation are closer to real matches. The players grasp more quickly how movements can be used in real match situations.

Tips:
- See the tips for individual drills.
- Ensure that the location on the field is appropriate.
- Choose the right direction of play. Try to organize the drill so that it is carried out in the direction of the fixed goal. In some cases (larger groups, more repetitions), the drill can also be carried out in other directions.
- Take account of the positions of the (virtual) defenders. The defender is usually inside the winger.
- Ensure that the technique or movement is executed with the right attitude.
- Ensure that the drill can be developed into a 1v1 situation.
- Ensure that the follow-up corresponds to the location on the field. A central attacker's run will often be followed by a shot at goal.
- The execution of the movement must serve the aims of the game. Taking the ball past an opponent must guarantee that a chance is created or a goal is scored.

Example of a functional drill:

Opponent behind
The players practice the following movements:
- Turning immediately
- Receiving, faking and turning
- Drawing an opponent to one side

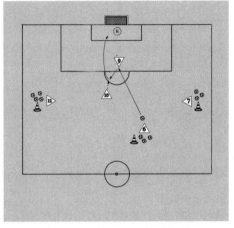

Organization:
The striker (9) and the withdrawn striker (10) stand on the edge of the penalty area. The striker calls for the ball, receives it with his back to the goal, turns, fakes, dribbles past his opponent and shoots at goal. This is repeated another 5 times then the withdrawn striker takes the place of the striker.

Variations:
- The striker stands with his back to the goal. The withdrawn striker faces the goal. The striker turns away or lays the ball off to the supporting withdrawn striker.
- Both players stand with their back to goal. One runs toward the ball and the other runs away from it. Turn or lay-off.
- With one defender.

Coaching:
- Allow the players the freedom to practice as they want.
- See tips for 1v1 situations with a defender behind.

Opponent in front

The players practice the following movements:
- Dragging inside
- Inside – outside
- Double scissor

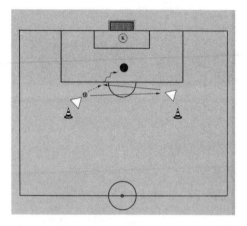

Organization:
- Two attackers pass the ball to each other.
- The defender takes up positions relative to the ball.
- One of the attackers can receive the ball and dribble past the defender.
- The defender has a passive role but exerts as much pressure as possible.

Note:
The defender must continuously adjust his position as the attackers pass the ball to each other. The attackers therefore experience 1v1 situations in a variety of positions, so that the drill simulates 'real' match conditions more closely.

Variation:
This drill can be developed into a real 1v1 situation.

Coaching:
Approach the defender directly or draw him toward one side.

Step 3: 1v1 with a "handicapped" defender

A handicapped defender is a line defender, a zone defender or a defender with a disadvantage relative to his opponent (e.g. distance from his opponent). If the players can move directly from practicing a technique or movement to a 1v1 situation, this phase is unnecessary. A handicapped defender can always be introduced if the players are not very successful when they try out a newly acquired technique. Handicapping the defender gives the attacker a better chance of using a movement successfully. A handicapped defender is especially useful when players are practicing 1v1 with a defender in front or a defender behind.

Tips:
- The resistance offered by the defender can be gradually increased.
- Ensure that the defender has a realistic chance of winning the ball.
- Ensure that the defender can score a goal if he wins the ball.
- The defender's position should be the same as his position in a real match.
- A handicapped defender can play in combination with a non-handicapped defender.
- Don't spend too long on this phase. Move on to 1v1 situations involving "real" defenders as soon as possible.

Examples of drills with a handicapped defender:

Defender behind
The players practice the following movements:
- Turning immediately
- Receiving, faking and turning
- Drawing an opponent to one side

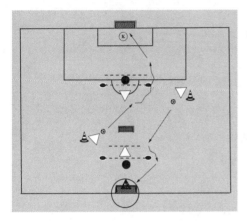

Organization:
- Both attackers receive passes when they have a defender immediately behind them
- At the moment when the ball is passed to the attacker, the defender must touch one of the two spots (flat cones) with his foot.
- A defender can score in the small goal.
- An attacker can score in the large goal defended by a goalkeeper.

Coaching:
- See tips for 1v1 situations with a defender behind.

Opponent in front
The players practice the following movements:

- Inside – stepover - outside
- Scissor to the inside
- Stepover to the outside

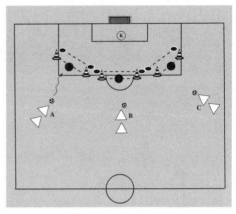

Organization:
- The players take turns at confronting a line defender in a 1v1 situation.
- If the defender wins the ball, the players swap roles.
- If the attacker takes the ball past the defender and takes the ball directly over the imaginary line, the defender has to do 10 push-ups.
- When an attacker scores, he moves on to the next group (A to B, B to C, C to A).

Variation:
- This drill can be developed further.
- 2 line defenders in sequence.
- 1 line defender and 1 zonal defender in sequence.
- 1 zonal defender
- 1v1

Coaching:
See coaching points for 1v1 situations with an opponent in front.

Step 4: 1v1

Training for 1v1 situations is a core part of learning the movements needed to dribble and turn past an opponent. When the functional aspects of the movements have been learned, the 1v1 situation is the most important follow-up step. The aim must always be to bring out the relevance to real match situations. The direction of play, the location on the field and the relationship to a situation on the field can put a movement or technique into the right context. The coach must find situations that are suitable for making things clear to the players.

Tips:
- Start from the attacker's position or a real match situation.
- Ensure that the opposition can also score.
- Ensure a good work/rest balance.
- Ensure that the situation is in the right part of the field.
- Pay attention to the direction of the play. The attacker should play toward the fixed goal.
- Encourage players to be themselves. Encourage the players to try out their turning movements and fakes.
- Ensure that the defender's position corresponds to his position in a real match.
- Build up to 2v1 and 2v2 if possible.
- Encourage the players; coach positively.
- If the attackers dribble past the defenders too easily, the coach must encourage the defenders. The obstacles in the drills must correspond to obstacles encountered in real matches.

Examples of 1v1 drills

Defender behind
The players practice the following movements:
- Turning immediately
- Receiving, faking and turning
- Drawing an opponent to one side

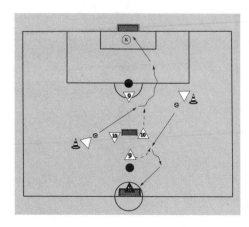

Organization:
- The striker (9) receives a pass in front of the goal.
- The striker can turn away from the defender or lay the ball off with his first touch to the supporting withdrawn striker (10).
- The withdrawn striker must shoot first time.

In effect this is a 2v1 situation. However, if only 2 players are involved it is obvious that the striker will turn away, so the situation bears no resemblance to reality.

Coaching:
See tips for 1v1 situations with a defender behind.

Defender in front

The players practice the following move-
ments:
- Inside – stepover - outside
- Scissor to the inside
- Stepover to the outside

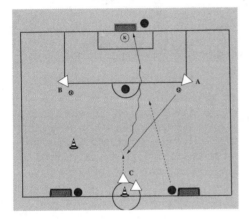

Organization:
- Player A passes to player C.
- Player C receives the ball and confronts the
  defender in front of goal (1v1).
- At the moment when player C receives the
  ball, the second defender can join in and
  exert pressure.
- Player C can score in the large goal, and the
  defender can score in one of the small goals.
- The 2 defenders swap places.
- Player B starts the sequence again.

Involving a second defender is a way of forc-
ing the attacker to act more quickly. In effect,
however, this remains a 1v1 situation (adjust
the distance from the second defender).

Coaching:
See tips for 1v1 situations with a defender
behind.

Step 5: Application of skills in a match situation

The application of the movements needed
to dribble past an opponent and 1v1 skills in
match situations is often neglected. Unless
they are used in match situations, however,
they cannot be fully exploited. Placing movements or situations in a match context brings
about a transfer of these skills.

Movements can best be put into practice in
small drills with lots of repetition. Match-related drills such as 3v3, 4v4 and 5v5 are ideal
for coupling the technical aspect to insight.
The tactical aspects come more to the fore in
match-related drills involving more players (7v7, 8v8). In particular, the "where" and
"when" aspects can be worked out.

The content of the drills need not always be
oriented toward the fakes and tricks needed
to dribble past an opponent. As indicated in
the introduction, the movements are a means
for achieving the aims of the game. The coach
can offer advice about movements at appropriate moments during match-related drills.

Encouraging ball skills in match-related drills by means of:
- success moments
- tasks
- the organization of the drill

Example:

Rewards
Taking the ball past an opponent in the penalty area and scoring = goal counts double.

Task
1v1 situation with opponent behind
The defenders are given the task of getting in
front of the attackers as often as possible. This
gives the attackers the opportunity to turn
away to one side.

81

1v1 situation with opponent in front

The team in possession is told to leave the striker sufficient space for an individual run when the team is in possession.

Organization:
The striker can score by running with the ball over the line. A number of situations arise in which the attacker has to take the ball past an opponent.

> *An enjoyable task at the end of the training session. If you can tunnel your direct opponent (i.e. send the ball through his legs), he has to leave the field. Who is first to score 5 goals?*

Tips:
- Players must not run with the ball just for the sake of it.
- Avoid setting artificial tasks.
- Don't forget the 'free' play.

Tips for coaching 1v1 situations with opponent in front or opponent behind

In view of the importance of being able to take the ball past an opponent down the center of the field, I have collected the most important tips. They are divided into 2 groups:
- coaching of movements
- coaching of 1v1 situations

Coaching of movements for dribbling past an opponent

When coaching movements for dribbling past an opponent, it is important to start from the player's individual qualities. Each player has his own style of dribbling. When players are introduced to a drill, movement or situation, they should be given the time to discover what it is about. During this discovery phase (in which the players freely practice the movement), the coach has the time to analyze the players individual qualities. He can then take these into consideration as the training session proceeds. It is also good if a coach uses players' successes to illustrate his talks or demonstrations.

Some tips
Right attitude

When players practice a movement, they do not always do so with the right attitude. The drills are often carried out sluggishly, with little variation in pace. In the first phase it is important for the players to acquire the necessary coordination to master a movement. It is pointless to ask them to speed up if they have not yet mastered the necessary technique.

When the players are in control of the ball, the intensity of the drill can be increased. This is the moment when the importance of a correct attitude should be emphasized. As their attitude changes and they become more determined, their technical skills come under more pressure. If the players carry out movements and techniques too sluggishly and with too little conviction, this will be reflected in match-related drills later.

Tips:
- Increase the ball tempo – ensure that the (virtual) defender is put under pressure.
- Cultivate a winning mentality.
- Carry out movements with conviction.

Ensure that the first touch is good

Ball control is often a major obstacle in a real match. Pressure can also be exerted in simulated competitive situations. You often see players set off on a run from a stationary position. This rarely occurs in a real match. Confronting players with a variety of match-related passes (pass along the ground, pass through the air) forces them to develop their coordinative skills (receive with the first touch; go with the second touch).

- When you receive the ball, try to control it in such a way that you can go forward.
- Touch the ball frequently as you run with it, so that you can react quickly if challenged.
- Try to control the ball with your first touch so that you can play it in the direction you want with your second touch.
- Do not deviate too far from the straightest line to the goal.

Remain as central as possible in front of goal

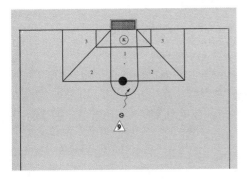

In a 1v1 situation with the opponent in front, the attacker must remain as central as possible in front of goal. This is the position in which he is most dangerous. If the attacker is forced away from this position (toward zones 2 or 3), it is more difficult to score and the attacker will be forced to pass to a teammate who is in a better position.

Be forceful

Increasing the speed of the drills forces the players to act faster. This stimulates their skills and brings their speed of action closer to the level needed in 'real' 1v1 situations. If the players are allowed to slow down the pace of the drills, this will be reflected in 1v1 situations.

- The attacker dictates the tempo, not the defender (keep the defender under pressure).

Go directly toward the defender or draw him to the right or the left.

There are two ways to take the ball past an opponent:
Take the ball directly toward him.

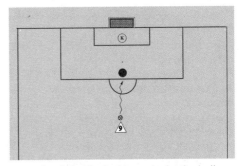

Draw the defender inside and take the ball past him on the outside, or vice versa.

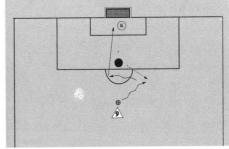

The choice is usually made on the basis of insight. The coach can, however, devote time to specific skills.

Use your body to fake to the side.

Tips:
- Keep your knees slightly bent (lower center of gravity).
- The fake comes mainly from the upper half of your body.

Time the body swerve or fake or trick properly

It is important to learn when to carry out a movement. Ideally this should be practiced against a real defender, but a cone or a line or a gate can also be used to help players estimate distances.

Tips:
- Start the movement at a sufficient distance from the defender.
- Take the initiative or wait for a reaction from the defender.

Accelerate after dribbling past your opponent

The player's attitude is decisive here. If the player does not accelerate after dribbling the ball past a virtual defender, this will be reflected in 1v1 situations. After a player dribbles past a cone, he must accelerate.

What is the next step after going past an opponent?

Dribbling the ball past an opponent should not be an aim in itself. It must be done for a purpose. The player should know what he wants to do after leaving his opponent behind him.

Tips:
- Remain focused after dribbling past an opponent.
- Be aware of the situation around you.
- Run with the ball, shoot at goal, pass to a teammate, cross the ball.

Coaching 1v1 situations

Here, too, it is interesting to establish a framework. Again, it is important to start from the player's individual qualities. A coach can learn useful information simply by allowing the players to follow their inclination for a while. Some players have specific movements for taking the ball past an opponent. Other simply rely on speed. Each player's abilities must be analyzed. The coach can then decide what approach to take. A player who relies on speed will sooner or later come up against problems. By encouraging him to practice certain effective movements and giving him a better insight into 1v1 situations, the coach prepares him for the future.

Start from the player's individual qualities.

Right attitude

In a 1v1 situation, one player has to overcome the other. By approaching the situation with the right attitude, an attacker forces his opponent onto the defensive.

- Dare to take on the defender!
- Want to win!
- Don't be put off!

The first touch is important!

Controlling the ball under pressure from an opponent is difficult. The position of the opponent influences the way the ball is controlled.
- Try to control the ball in such a way that you can go forward.
- Keep the ball away from your opponent.
- Touch the ball as often as you can, so that you can react quickly if your opponent challenges.

Dribbling past an opponent
Option 1: Put pressure on your opponent
Maintaining a fast pace puts pressure on an opponent. He therefore loses the initiative in a 1v1 situation.
- Maintain a fast pace. Make the defender move.
- The attacker dictates the pace, not the defender (maintain pressure on the defender).

Option 2: Switch from slow to fast
Approach your opponent with the ball at your feet. A soon as your opponent slows his pace, make your move to go past him. The sudden switch from slow to fast takes the defender by surprise.

Go toward your opponent and draw him to the right or left
The player with the ball decides how to go past his opponent. Drawing an opponent to one side or the other is a question of insight. The skill level of the player is also a factor. Some players can dribble past a defender more easily on the inside, and some on the outside. The skill level of the defender is also an important aspect. Older players in particular must learn how to size up an opponent as part of their development.

Drawing a defender:

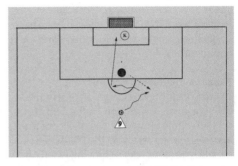

Draw the defender in a given direction by taking the ball in that direction. The defender has to move to cover the attacker's path. As the defender moves, the attacker can take the ball past him in the other direction.

Approach the defender directly

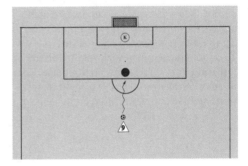

There are two options:
a) Maintain a fast pace and make the defender move.
b) Suddenly switch from slow to fast.

Use your body when you fake

Using the whole body to make a fake is above all an African/Brazilian specialty. A fake requires more than just leg movement. The upper body plays a key role in deceiving an opponent.

Time the movement properly

The timing of the fake depends on a number of factors. The position on the field, the position of the opponent, the quality of the first touch when receiving the ball, whether the player is stationary or moving when he receives the ball, etc. Sometimes an attacker has very little time to make a movement. By practicing 1v1 challenges frequently, the attacker learns to estimate distances and to time his movements properly.

Accelerate after making a fake

In this early phase, players frequently lose possession. It is important to follow a fake with a decisive run. Appropriate movements and acceleration are essential in order to get past an opponent. In practice, players are often not fast enough to dribble past an opponent. The attacker frequently takes the ball too close to the defender, and as a result it is intercepted.

Cut across the line of the defender's run if possible

What happens after the ball is taken past the defender?

It is important that the player with the ball remains aware of the situation around him after he goes past an opponent. This situation makes a lot of demands on his insight and technique. Adapting the follow-up action (a cross or a shot at goal) to situations that occur in real matches improves the outcomes of 1v1 situations in such matches.

> "Players think too often about passing, passing, passing ..."
>
> *Réné Meulensteen, Skills Development Coach*
> *Manchester United*

1v1 situation with opponent behind

Practicing fakes and dribbling movements

Here too, it is important to analyze the individuality of the players. In principle the same tips apply as for the 1v1 situation with an opponent in front.

Right attitude

Attackers are often not sufficiently dynamic when they turn away from an opponent. They therefore face problems when they are confronted by real defenders.

Remain as central as possible in front of goal

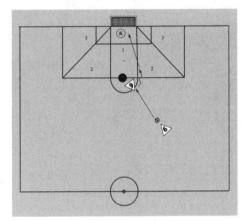

Here, too, it is essential that an attacker does not allow himself to be forced too far away from a central position in front of goal.

Be forceful

There are 3 ways of making yourself available to receive a pass

Run straight toward the ball

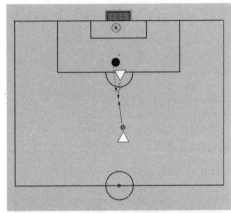

The attacker runs straight toward the ball, followed closely by his marker. The attacker can lay the ball off, control it or turn with the ball in one movement as he receives it.

Run diagonally toward the ball

Drawing the defender out of position

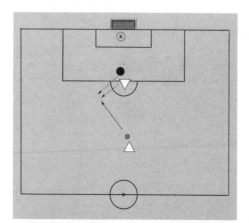

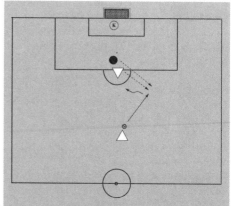

The attacker runs diagonally toward the ball. The defender must decide whether or not to follow him. The attacker can turn toward the flank, turn away, hold the ball or lay the ball off.

The attacker runs diagonally toward the ball, hoping to draw the defender after him. When the defender is close to him, the attacker can lay the ball off, hold the ball or turn away in the opposite direction.

The attacker can turn away in two ways:

Hold the ball and fake

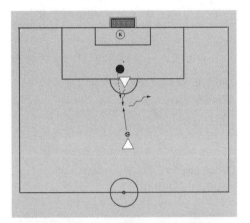

The attacker receives the ball and tries to deceive the defender with a fake before turning away from him with the ball.

Turning away in one movement

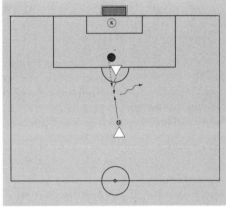

The attacker turns away immediately from the defender in one movement as he receives the ball.

Use your body
Tips:
In some cases, using your body can make turning away from an opponent easier.

> "Ronaldo uses your body if you get too close to him. He is broad and just turns round you."
>
> *Thuram, France*

Tips:
Use your body when you fake
Keep your knees slightly bent (lower center of gravity). This helps you to move more easily and faster.

Stand at an angle
If an attacker stands at an angle he can turn away from his opponent more quickly.

Accelerate after a fake or after dribbling past your opponent

The player's attitude is decisive here. If the player does not accelerate after dribbling the ball past a virtual defender, this will be reflected in 1v1 situations. After a player turns away from a defender he must accelerate.

What is the next step after going past an opponent?
Dribbling the ball past an opponent should not be an aim in itself. It must be done for a purpose. The player should know what he wants to do after leaving his opponent behind him.

Tips:
- Remain focused after dribbling past an opponent.
- Be aware of the situation around you.
- Run with the ball, shoot at goal, pass to a teammate, cross the ball.

Coaching 1v1 situations with an opponent behind

Right attitude
In a 1v1 situation, one player has to overcome the other. By approaching the situation with the right attitude, an attacker forces his opponent onto the defensive.

Dare to take the ball past an opponent
Players must have the attitude that nothing can stop them.

Glance over your shoulder
If you do this you know exactly where your opponent is.

Don't always choose the same run line
Surprise your opponent by sometimes running diagonally toward the ball.

Feel where your opponent is
In some situations (e.g. in the penalty area), there is close contact with your opponent. It is important to use both hands to 'feel' exactly where your opponent is.

Good first touch
When you turn away from an opponent it is important that the first touch takes the ball in the right direction.

Ensure that the ball can immediately be played in the right direction
Keep the ball away from the defender.

Don't be predictable
An attacker who always received the ball in the same way is easier to defend against. It is important to put the defender under pressure. An attacker who always threatens to turn away from his marker and make forward runs often has more time on the ball. His marker is less inclined to take risks in trying to win the ball.

Screen the ball with your body
The ability to use your body in a 1v1 situation is crucial.

Do not stand still as you receive the ball
The defender must not be given any opportunity to win the ball. It is therefore important that the attacker remains keeps moving as he receives the ball.

Use your body when you fake
The defender cannot always see exactly where the ball is. If you fake with your upper body there is more chance that the defender will be deceived.

Accelerate after a fake or after dribbling past your opponent
When you turn away from an opponent it is important to accelerate in order to leave him behind.

Cut across the run line of the defender if possible

What is the next step after going past an opponent?
After turning away from an opponent it is important to maintain an overview. A player is often so focused on challenging for and winning the ball that he lacks the necessary composure after shaking off his opponent. Especially in front of goal, players are not calm enough to assess the situation properly.

"You can dance all you want, but when Roy Keane wants the ball, he'll get it. When you do a trick, do it quickly."

Mick Priest, Youth Coach
Manchester United

COACHING METHOD
Coaching the aims of the game and soccer problems

10 to 14-year olds

COACHING THE AIMS OF THE GAME

Tips for 10 to 14-year olds:

The players

10 to 12-year-olds: At this age we talk more about passing to the striker and withdrawn striker individually. The players in this age group are in the process of becoming accustomed to 11v11. There is as yet no sign of genuine teamwork. Attackers need time and space to find their way in the larger playing field. Experimenting with running with the ball, combination plays, etc. are all part of this phase. Typical coaching points should be put forward but not imposed. The emphasis is more on individual interpretation.

13 and 14-year-olds: Players in this age group have advanced sufficiently to be receptive to coaching about the interplay between the striker and withdrawn striker and other players. The build-up to an attack proceeds more smoothly and can be more easily influenced. The naïve approach of the 10 to 12-year-olds is replaced by more realism. The players have a better insight and more attention can be paid to movement off the ball.

Training sessions

In the first phase we choose drills up to 5v5 (positional training) or a passing and shooting drill. All aspects of the striker's and withdrawn striker's positions are handled. The 1v1 situation in a variety of positions (opponent behind – forward pass) plays an important role.

In the second phase we train with 2 lines. These may be attackers and midfielders or defenders and attackers. Drills up to 7v8 are ideal for this. We end the session with 8v8 or 11v11 (possibly against players in an older or younger group).

10 to 12-year-olds: Taking the ball past an opponent and dominating an opponent play an important role. Nothing is forced at this age. The players are given coaching points and simply set about putting them into practice. The quickest way of influencing

them is positional training (from 2v1 to 5v4). The attackers have a lot of ball contacts and a lot of scoring chances. The best method of preparing the players for 11v11 is to train with 2 lines (from 6v4 to 8v7). These drills are closer to real game situations. The focus at this age is mainly on technical skills and the challenges encountered in real games (shooting, turning and shooting, taking the ball past an opponent). All skills that can be carried out over short distances can be practiced fully.

13 and 14-year-olds: After the emphasis on positional training in the 10 to 12-year-old group, the 13 and 14-year-olds focus more on drills with 2 lines involving more players. The players have made the transition to 11v11 and are ready for more detailed development. In this age group, attackers are used more as target players and intermediate players. Drills involving passes over longer distances (with teammates moving up in support) are ideal. 1v1 remains a key aspect, with more attention being given to choosing the right moment to make a run with the ball. More direction is introduced, without losing the unforced element completely.

The coach

The tasks and function of the striker are relatively clear to the coach. The tasks and function of the withdrawn striker are less clear. The action radius of the withdrawn striker is between the midfield and the attack. This position is not always easy to describe to young players. Coaching points should be chosen to suit the qualities of the individual players.

10 to 12-year-olds: The coaching of 10 to 12-year-olds should be totally relaxed. Players cannot be put under pressure at this age. The coach analyzes the individual performances of his players, identifies their strong and weak points and tries to encourage them by offering targeted coaching points. The attackers are given space to experiment in different situations.

13 and 14-year-olds: A more detailed approach is taken at this age. There are clear guidelines for the attackers. The creation of chances is clearly explained. Within the constraints of these guidelines the coach creates sufficient freedom. The coach tries to position the training at the limits of the players' capabilities. He sets challenges to promote the players' progress. Despite the more structured approach, the players must still be able to enjoy the coaching sessions.

The match

10 to 12-year-olds: The action radius of the players is limited. The play therefore seems to be more technical. The players always seek solutions that are close at hand. Passes to attackers often come from the midfield. In view of the limited action radius, the players are often too close to each other. The attackers must learn how to position themselves when their team is in possession.

13 and 14-year olds: The transition from build-up to attack is more mature. The players are able to miss out one line in the build-up. In general, the players' action radius is greater. Passes are made over longer distances, resulting in more options.

Aim

The central attack module for 10 to 14-year-olds
Aim: To learn 11v11
"Learning to cope with match-related obstacles"
Own position – 2 lines

Drills:

Discovery phase

Passing and shooting drill
Ball skills drill
1v1 drill

Positional training

2 : 1 =>
2 : 2 =>
3 : 2 =>
3 : 2 =>
3 : 3 =>
4 : 2 =>
4 : 3 =>
4 : 4 =>
5 : 4 =>

Line training, 2 lines

5 : 4 =>
5 : 5 =>
6 : 4 =>
6 : 5 =>
6 : 6 =>
7 : 5 =>
7 : 6 =>
7 : 7 =>
8 : 7 =>

Training phase

Positional training

2 : 1 =>
2 : 2 =>
3 : 2 =>
3 : 2 =>
3 : 3 =>
4 : 2 =>
4 : 3 =>
4 : 4 =>
5 : 4 =>

Line training, 2 lines

5 : 4 =>
5 : 5 =>
6 : 4 =>
6 : 5 =>
6 : 6 =>
7 : 5 =>
7 : 6 =>
7 : 7 =>
8 : 7 =>

Game phase

Match-related drill (8v8 or 11v11)

Practical example:
Learning one of the aims of the game

Young players do not have much insight when they play 11v11. They need to develop further before they can play in a 1-3-4-3 formation. We therefore speak of learning one of the aims of the game in this age group. The players learn the principles of one of the aims of the game.

Learning one of the aims of the game

We have chosen the following sequence for the players to learn one of the aims of the game.

We determine:

The starting situation
The age group
The level
The number of training sessions per week
The starting level of the players

The development objective
What do we want to achieve?

We then choose the following steps:

1. What playing system are we going to choose?
2. Which module do we want to choose?
3. Which players are we looking at?
4. Which part of the field and in which direction?
5. What drills should we choose?
6. How should we factor in the age-typical aspects?
7. How should we draw up the schedule?
8. What should be the content of the training session?

We determine
The starting situation:

Age group: 10 and 11-year-olds
Level: Low amateur level
Number of training sessions per week: 2
Starting level of the players:
The players have no experience of attacking play in an 11v11 context.

The development objective:
Creating chances
1v1 variations in attack with an opponent behind
Encouraging interplay between the attackers

1. What playing system are we going to choose?
The players in this age group play in a 1-3-4-3 formation.

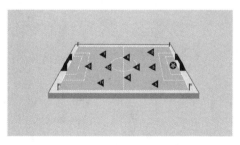

2. Which module do we want to choose?
The central attack module.

3. Which players are we looking at?

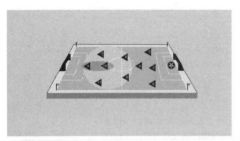

Primarily the striker (9) and the withdrawn striker (10) in combination with the wingers (7 and 11), the midfielders (6 and 8) and some-times the full backs (2 and 5).

4. Which part of the field and in which direction?

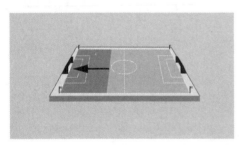

In the opposing team's half, in the direction of the opposing team's goal.

5. What drills should we choose?

- Passing and shooting drills.
- Ball skill drills
- 1v1 drills
- Positional training (from 2v1 to 5v5).
- Line training with 2 lines (from 5v5 to 8v8).

Passing and shooting drills are useful for focusing on technical aspects. Positional training and drills with 2 lines are eminently suitable for coaching how the striker and the withdrawn striker combine with the other players. Ball skill drills can emphasize typical skills for attacking play. 1v1 drills are ideal for putting these skills into practice in real games. 2v1 to 5v5 drills (positional training) are im-portant for the coaching of easily understand-able situations. Drills with 2 lines are good for coaching how the attackers and the midfield-ers or defenders should combine.

6. How should we factor in the age-typical aspects?

The 10 to 14 age group is in the learning phase for 11v11. Besides developing general skills, it is important to put the players more or less in their own positions. There is not much point in placing defenders in attack-ing positions when coaching attacking play. The players have a lot of time necessary just to absorb the developments relating to their own position and capabilities.

In the first phase it is better to coach the striker and withdrawn striker separately. The interplay between the two players can be focused on at a later stage.

7. How should we draw up the schedule?

This schedule is simply an example. Coaches should not simply copy it. Factors such as enthusiasm, form on the day, the translation of the aim of the game in practice and the time of year all influence the scheduling of the training sessions. Coaches must translate the aim of the game into practice in ways that suit their own situation.

Tuesday	training	tactical	attack module	session 1
Thursday	training	Practicing technique in 1v1 situations with defender behind		
Saturday	match			
Tuesday	training	tactical	attack module	session 2
Thursday	training	tactical	attack module	session 3
Saturday	match			
Tuesday	training	tournament drill (4v4)		
Thursday	training	tactical	attack module	session 4
Saturday	match			

8. What should be the content of the training session?

The development objectives of the sessions:

Session 1: We start with a passing and shooting drill which includes all ways of turning away. In the training phase we couple technique to insight: the players are confronted with a 2v1 situation. We finish the session with a match-related drill of 5v5. This guarantees lots of repetition.

Session 2: In the discovery phase we again have the 2v1 situation from the previous session. This is then expanded to 2v2 + goalkeeper with a handicapped defender. This guarantees the two attackers' chances of scoring. In the training phase we have 4v2 + goalkeeper. We again finish with a match-related drill of 5v5.

Session 3: We repeat the passing and shooting drill from session 1. We then have 2v2 + goalkeeper with a handicapped defender. In the training phase we have 4v2 + goalkeeper. If possible we develop this to 4v3 + goalkeeper. We again finish with a match-related drill of 5v5.

Session 4: In the discovery phase we expand the 2v2 situation. A midfielder can join in after the ball is passed (3v2 + goalkeeper). In the training phase we go on with 4v3 + goalkeeper. When the players have made sufficient progress the drill can be developed to 4v4 + goalkeeper. We finish with a match-related drill of 8v8.

Session 1
Development objective of the session
We start with a passing and shooting drill which includes all ways of turning away. In the training phase we couple technique to insight: the players are confronted with a 2v1 situation. We finish the session with a match-related drill of 5v5. This guarantees lots of repetition.

Discovery phase: Passing and shooting drill
                    – turning away from an
                    opponent
Training phase: 2v1 + K
Game phase: Match-related drill (5v5,
                    depending on the number
                    of available players)

Content of the session
Discovery phase:
Passing and shooting drill – turning away from an opponent

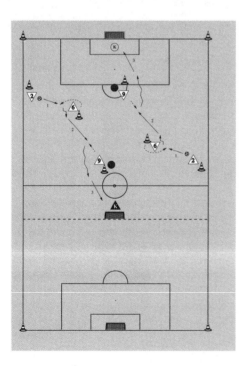

Organization:
The right back (2) passes to the right midfielder (6). The right midfielder turns and passes to the striker (9). The striker turns and shoots. The players all move up one position. The full back becomes the midfielder, the midfielder becomes the striker and the striker joins in on the other side of the field as the full back.

Variations:
- Turn away with the first touch
- Control the ball and turn away.
- Draw the defender to one side (the coach can position a cone as a guide point)
- 2v1 (a withdrawn striker joins in)
  - Attackers can score in the large goal
  - The Defender can score in the small goal

Coaching points:
Position of defenders (2 and 5)
- Pass as far forward as possible to the midfielder
- Pass the ball firmly
- Communicate with the midfielder

Position of midfielders (6 and 8)
- Feel where the opposing player is or look over your shoulder
- Be aware of the position of the player behind you
- Play the ball away from the defender
- Play the ball in firmly so that the attacker can turn with it more easily.

Striker (9)
- Feel where the opposing player is or look over your shoulder
- Turn away explosively
- Shoot as quickly as possible

Training phase: positional play 2v1+K

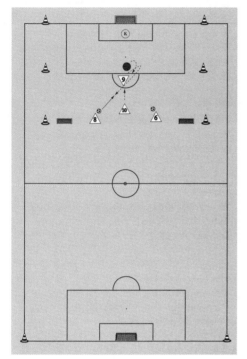

Organization:
- The striker (9) calls for the ball from one of the midfielders (6 or 8).
- At the moment when the striker calls 'play,' one of the midfielders passes to him.
- The withdrawn striker (10) then moves up in support.
- Attackers can score in the large goal.
- Defenders can score in one of the small goals.

Coaching points:
Striker (9)
- Feel where the opposing player is or look over your shoulder
- Lay the ball off or turn away from the opposing player

Withdrawn striker (10)
- Move up in support as quickly as possible
- Vary your run line (toward the striker, across behind the striker, etc.)

Success moment:
5 attempts – 3 of them must result in a goal.

Game phase:
5v5 (depending on the number of available players).

Session 2
Development objective of the session
In the discovery phase we again have the 2v1 situation from the previous session. This is then expanded to 2v2 + goalkeeper with a handicapped defender. This guarantees the two attackers' chances of scoring. In the training phase we have 4v2 + goalkeeper. We again finish with a match-related drill of 5v5.

Discovery phase:	2v1 + K – 2v2 + K
Training phase:	4v2 + K
Game phase:	Match-related drill (5v5, depending on the number of available players)

Content of the session
Discovery phase:
2v1 + K – 2v2 + K

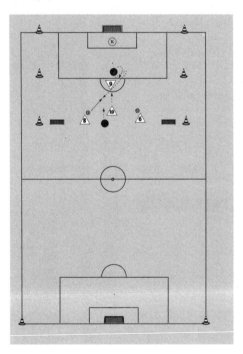

Organization:
- The striker (9) calls for the ball from one of the midfielders (6 or 8).
- At the moment when the striker calls 'play,' one of the midfielders passes to him.
- The withdrawn striker (10) then moves up in support.
- Attackers can score in the large goal.
- Defenders can score in one of the small goals.
- The drill is expanded to 2v2 + goalkeeper. When the pass is played to the striker, a second defender can join in.

Coaching points:
Striker (9)
- Feel where the opposing player is or look over your shoulder
- Lay the ball off or turn away from the opposing player

Withdrawn striker (10)
- Move up in support as quickly as possible
- Vary your run line (toward the striker, across behind the striker, etc.)

Success moment:
5 attempts – 3 of them must result in a goal.

Training phase: 4v2+K

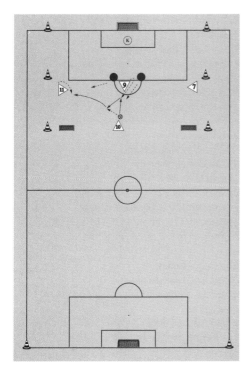

Organization:
- We play 4v2 + goalkeeper
- Attackers can score in the large goal.
- Defenders can score in one of the small goals.

Coaching points:
Striker (9)
- Feel where the opposing player is or look over your shoulder
- Lay the ball off or turn away from the opposing player

Withdrawn striker (10)
- Move up in support as quickly as possible
- Vary your run line (toward the striker, across behind the striker, etc.)

Success moment:
Change of positions when the defenders score twice.

Game phase:
5v5 (Depending on the number of available players.)

Session 3
Development objective of the session
Session 3: We repeat the passing and shooting drill from session 1. We then have 2v2 + goalkeeper with a handicapped defender. In the training phase we have 4v2 + goalkeeper. If possible we develop this to 4v3 + goalkeeper. We again finish with a match-related drill of 5v5.

Discovery phase:	Passing and shooting drill – turning away from an opponent
Training phase:	4v2 + K – 4v3 + K
Game phase:	Match-related drill (5v5, depending on the number of available players)

Content of the session
Discovery phase:
Passing and shooting drill – turning away from an opponent

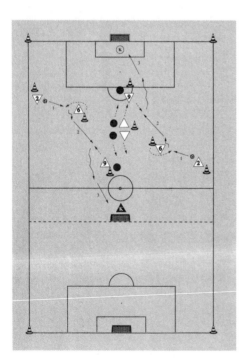

Organization:
- The right back (2) passes to the right midfielder (6).
- The right midfielder turns and passes to the striker (9).
- The striker turns and shoots.
- The players all move up one position. The full back becomes the midfielder, the midfielder becomes the striker and the striker joins in on the other side of the field as the full back.

Variations:
- Turn away with the first touch
- Control the ball and turn away.
- Draw the defender to one side (the coach can position a cone as a guide point)
- 2v1 (a withdrawn striker joins in)
  - Attackers can score in the large goal
  - The Defender can score in the small goal

Coaching points:
Position of defenders (2 and 5)
- Pass as far forward as possible to the midfielder
- Pass the ball firmly
- Communicate with the midfielder

Position of midfielders (6 and 8)
- Feel where the opposing player is or look over your shoulder
- Be aware of the position of the player behind you
- Play the ball away from the defender
- Play the ball in firmly so that the attacker can turn with it more easily.

Striker (9)
- Feel where the opposing player is or look over your shoulder
- Turn away explosively
- Shoot as quickly as possible

Training phase: 4v2 + K – 4v3 + K

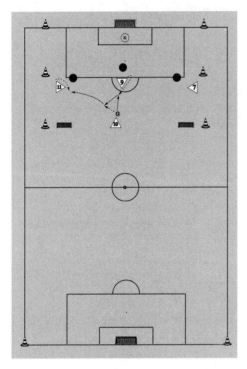

Organization:
- We play 4v2 + goalkeeper or 4v3 + goal-keeper
- Attackers can score in the large goal.
- Defenders can score in one of the small goals.

Coaching points:
Striker (9)
- Feel where the opposing player is or look over your shoulder
- Lay the ball off or turn away from the opposing player

Withdrawn striker (10)
- Move up in support as quickly as possible
- Vary your run line (toward the striker, across behind the striker, etc.)

Success moment:
Change of positions when the defenders score twice.

Game phase:
5v5 (Depending on the number of available players.)

Session 4
Development objective of the session
Session 4: In the discovery phase we expand
the 2v2 situation. A midfielder can join in after
the ball is passed (3v2 + goalkeeper). In the
training phase we go on with 4v3 + goalkeeper. When the players have made sufficient
progress the drill can be developed to 4v4 +
goalkeeper. We finish with a match-related
drill of 8v8.

Discovery phase:	3v2 + K
Training phase:	4v3 + K – 4v4 + K
Game phase:	Match-related drill (8v8, depending on the number of available players)

Content of the session
Discovery phase:
3v2 + K

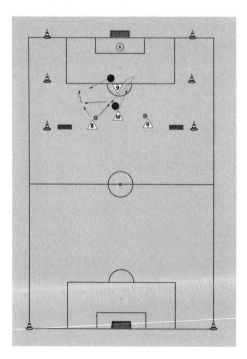

Organization:
- The striker (9) calls for the ball from one of
  the midfielders (6 or 8).
- The withdrawn striker (10) and the midfield-
  er then move up in support.
- Attackers can score in the large goal.
- Defenders can score in one of the small
  goals.

Coaching Points:
Striker (9)
- Feel where the opposing player is or look
  over your shoulder
- Lay the ball off or turn away from the oppos-
  ing player

Withdrawn striker (10)
- Move up in support as quickly as possible
- Vary your run line (toward the striker, across
  behind the striker, etc.)

Midfielder (6 or 8)
- Help the other players; support them.
- Do not get ahead of the ball too often.

Success moment:
5 attempts – 3 of them must result in a goal.

Training phase: 4v3 + K – 4v4 + K

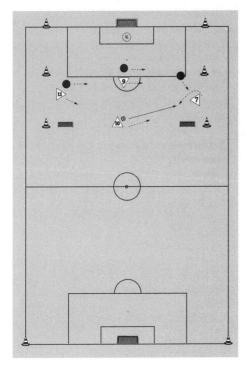

Organization:
- We play 4v3 + goalkeeper or 4v4 + goal-keeper
- Attackers can score in the large goal.
- Defenders can score in one of the small goals.

Coaching points:
Striker (9)
- Feel where the opposing player is or look over your shoulder
- Lay the ball off or turn away from the opposing player

Withdrawn striker (10)
- Move up in support as quickly as possible
- Vary your run line (toward the striker, across behind the striker, etc.)

Success moment:
The striker's goals count double.

Game phase:
8v8 (Depending on the number of available players.)

Evaluation

Coaching the aims of the game

- **Do the players enjoy themselves?**
  There is sufficient variation in the drills (match-related drills, finishing).

- **Is the development objective achieved?**
  The players' performance in real matches demonstrates that they have been influenced. The players show more initiative on the attacking moves. Clear progress has been made in the development objectives:
  - The creation of chances
  - The variations of 1v1 in attack, with opposing player behind
  - Encouragement of interplay between the attackers

- **Is the number of practice drills in the training sessions limited?**
  There are a maximum of 3 drills in each training session.

- **Is the number of practice drills in the module limited?**
  A total of 4 practice drills are integrated in the module.

- **Is there a good balance between match-related and non-match-related drills?**
  The match-related drills dominate. The non-match-related drills such as passing and shooting drills with finishing are more supportive in nature.

- **Is there a progressive buildup over a certain period?**
  Four training sessions are completed over a period of 3 weeks.

- **Are there sufficient repetitions for the players?**
  All players are sufficiently involved in each drill.

- **Is sufficient consideration given to the age group of the players?**
  The drills used in these practical examples are oriented to the players' age group. The content is adjusted to the age of the players.

- **Are the drills adjusted to their level?**
  The drills are applicable at the higher regional level. If they are too difficult, the coach can easily adjust them.

- **Do the players have sufficient freedom of movement?**
  Sufficient free moments are incorporated.

14 to 18-year olds

PROBLEM ORIENTED COACHING

Tips for 14 to 18-year olds:

The players

In this age group, winning gains steadily in importance. Their play when in possession becomes more refined and this has consequences for the attackers. An attacker in this age group must be aware of his own strengths and weaknesses and those of the opposition. The way in which he is brought into the play also depends on his strengths and weaknesses. A target player, for instance, might be easier to reach than a small, mobile striker. The important thing is to train and perfect an attacker's own qualities.

15 and 16-year-olds: At this age, attackers want to follow their own inclinations and are sometimes reluctant to accept advice. More discipline is demanded of the players, and their functions are more clearly described. An attacker is expected to work together with other players, even if this means putting in more effort.

17 and 18-year olds: Players in this age group are a step further. The attackers must be able to understand individual tactical instructions and put them into practice in match situations. If the opposition's central defenders have problems with the space behind them, the positional play of the attackers must be oriented to this. Missing a chance has more impact than in the 10 to 14-year-old group.

Training sessions

Depending on the work items derived from the match, a choice can be made from passing and shooting drills, 1v1 drills, positional training and line training with 2 or 3 lines. In the initial phase of the attacking play module it is interesting to work with smaller drills in which all the aspects of the attacking play module can be intensively practiced. This can be combined with larger drills (e.g. with 2 lines). These can involve the midfielders and attackers. In the following phase, drills with 3 lines can be introduced. The training sessions can end with a small sided drill of 8v8 or 11v11.

The capabilities of the players approach those of adult players. All aspects of attacking play can be used. Long forward passes, passes from one flank to the other, and involvement of the third man in the center can all be incorporated.

> "I understand why a lot of time is devoted to individual and strength training at AC Milan. I have done away with the strength training here, though, because I need the time for other things."
>
> *Ron Jans*

15 and 16-year-olds: At this age, drills with 2 and 3 lines are most closely related to the level of insight of the players. Small drills (such as positional training and passing and shooting drills) are more repetitive and, thanks to the large number of repetitions, are eminently suited for situation and technique-based coaching. The attackers almost always play in their own positions during training sessions.

17 and 18-year-olds: The obstacles that the coach creates on the training field must simulate real match situations. The pressure on the defenders must be as intense as possible. The attackers must be prepared for play at the highest level. Attackers must be confronted with a variety of circumstances during training sessions. It is useful to assign defenders other tasks during the drills (covering in front of the attacker) and to allow the attacker to anticipate this. In 11v11 there are many instructive moments: drills with 3 lines are eminently suitable here.

The coach

The coach is very demanding. The players can no longer interpret their tasks and functions to suit themselves.

The players have sufficient insight. The coach puts forward solutions and the players put them into practice. At this age the interests of the team and the effectiveness of the players' actions take precedence. The attacker must choose carefully between making a run with the ball and involving his teammates in a combination play. The coach is aware of this process. He coaches, prompts and intervenes when necessary.

15 and 16-year-olds: At this age the players want to win. The coach can make use of this. Points awarded for finishing drills have a good effect. The players can be too tempestuous and wild in challenges in front of goal. An important aspect of the coaching of 15 and 16-year-olds is encouraging them to remain cool in front of goal and under pressure.

1v1 must take priority at all ages

17 and 18-year-olds: Attackers in this group must be ready to make the step up to the first team and to deal with the pressures associated with this. The coach's demanding approach must not cause the players to be too cautious. The players must continue to develop their creativity.

The match

The coach must base his prompting on the manner in which his team plays and how the opposition plays. How is the opposing team playing relative to his own team? How can we create space? What are our strengths and the strengths of our opponents? What are our weaknesses and the weaknesses and the weaknesses of our opponents? What are the specific qualities of the striker and withdrawn striker? His analyses must leave room for his players to use their initiative.

15 and 16-year-olds: he players are able to play to obtain a result. In comparison with 10 to 14-year-olds, the attackers have less and less space. The importance of acting quickly increases. Attackers need to use their skills more efficiently to create scoring chances.

17 and 18-year-olds: The organization of the team when in possession and not in possession is good. It is more difficult to create chances by forceful play. The best moment for an attacker to strike is when the opposing team loses possession.

Aim

> **The central attack module between 14 and 18**
>
> *Aim:*
> - *To perfect playing 11v11*
> - *To learn how to deal with the manner in which the opposition plays*
> - *Collective development with regard to*
>   - *the strengths and weaknesses of the players' own team and the opposition*
>   - *the players' own positions, the line, the total team*

Drills for the discovery phase

Passing and shooting Ball skills 1v1	Positional training	Line training 2 lines	Line training 3 lines
	2 : 1 =>	5 : 4 =>	8 : 6 =>
	2 : 2 =>	5 : 5 =>	8 : 7 =>
	3 : 2 =>	6 : 4 =>	8 : 8 =>
	3 : 3 =>	6 : 5 =>	9 : 6 =>
	4 : 3 =>	6 : 6 =>	9 : 7 =>
	4 : 4 =>	7 : 5 =>	9 : 8 =>
	5 : 4 =>	7 : 6 =>	9 : 9 =>
		7 : 7 =>	10 : 8 =>
		8 : 7 =>	10 : 9 =>
			10 : 10 =>
			11 : 10 =>

Training phase

Line training 2 lines	Line training 3 lines
6 : 4 =>	8 : 6 =>
6 : 5 =>	8 : 7 =>
6 : 6 =>	8 : 8 =>
7 : 5 =>	9 : 6 =>
7 : 6 =>	9 : 7 =>
7 : 7 =>	9 : 8 =>
8 : 7 =>	9 : 9 =>
	10 : 8 =>
	10 : 9 =>
	10 : 10 =>
	11 : 10 =>

Game phase

Match-related drills (8v8 to 11 v11, depending on number of available players)

Practical example

Problem-oriented coaching

As the players get older, we talk of "problem-oriented coaching". The players have played 11v11 for a number of years and have built up a basic knowledge of the manner of playing. The coach can therefore base his coaching more on real match situations. The players know the aims of the build-up play and the coach can treat them in more detail. If the players in this age group are not sufficiently advanced, the coach can focus on coaching the aims of the game (see example for 10 to 14 year-olds).

Problem-oriented coaching

Problem-oriented coaching involves the following steps.

First we determine:
- The starting situation
- The age group
- The level
- The number of training sessions per week
- The starting level of the players
- The soccer problem – who, what, where, when?
- The development objective – what do we want to achieve?

We then choose the following steps:
1. What playing system are we going to choose?
2. Which module do we want to choose?
3. Which players are we looking at?
4. Which part of the field and in which direction?
5. What drills should we choose?
6. How should we factor in the age-typical aspects?
7. How should we draw up the schedule?
8. What should be the content of the training session?

We determine

The starting situation:

Age group: 15 and 16 year olds
Level: Amateur level
Number of training sessions per week: 2
Starting level of the players: The players are familiar with attacking play. However, the level of the players is still limited.

Soccer problem

When the players pass to the attackers in the opposition's half, the ball is not often enough played long for the attackers to run onto. Neither the striker (9) nor the withdrawn striker (10) makes forward runs.

The development objective

To encourage the players to send long forward passes to the striker and the withdrawn striker.

1. What playing system are we going to choose?

The players are familiar with a 1-4-3-3 formation.

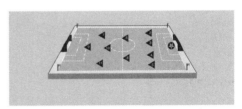

2. Which module do we want to choose?

The attacking play module.

3. Which players are we looking at?

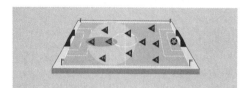

Mainly the striker (9), the withdrawn striker (10), the wingers (7 and 11) and the midfielders (6 and 8).

4. Which part of the field and in which direction?

In the opposition's half in the direction of the fixed goal.

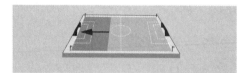

5. What drills should we choose?

The following drills can be used for the 14 to 18-year-old age group:
- Passing and shooting drills.
- Positional training (from 2v1 to 5v5).
- Line training with 2 lines (from 5v4 to 8v8).
- Line training with 3 lines (from 8v7 to 11v11).

6. How should we factor in the age-typical aspects?

In the oldest age group, the emphasis is on specialization in the player's own position. The positions that a player occupies during training sessions corresponds as far as possible to his strongest position.

7. How should we draw up the schedule?

The coach can put his own interpretation on this schedule.

Saturday – The match

During the match the coach is confronted with the following soccer problem: When the players pass to the attackers in the opposition's half, the ball is not often enough played long for the attackers to run onto. Neither the striker (9) nor the withdrawn striker (10) makes forward runs.

Tuesday	training	tactical	attack module session 1
Thursday	**training**	**tactical**	**attack module session 2**
Saturday	match	Both attackers show more initiative in the final third of the pitch, but the passing could be better.	
Tuesday	**training**	**tactical**	**attack module session 3**
Thursday	training	Positional play and match-related drill	
Saturday	match	The forward passing to the attackers is better. The players are showing more initiative.	
Tuesday	training	Finishing drill and match-related drill	
Thursday	**training**	**tactical**	**attack module session 4**
Saturday	match		

8. What should be the content of the training session?

We have devised 4 fictional training sessions.

The development objectives of the training sessions.

Session 1: This starts with a passing and shooting drill with the focus on forward runs. We then switch to a simple drill with 5v3 + goalkeeper, with the emphasis on getting the ball forward. We finish with a match-related drill (8v8).

Session 2: In session 2 we continue with the drill 5v3 + goalkeeper from the previous session. In the training phase we then expand this to 7v5 + goalkeeper. The emphasis here is on how the attackers and midfielders combine. We again finish with a match-related drill (8v8).

Session 3: Here we return to the passing and shooting drill. The players now know the aim. In the training phase, we switch to the drill with 2 lines (7v5 + goalkeeper). We finish with a match-related drill (8v8).

Session 4: We start the session again with positional training, but with an additional opponent this time (5v4 + goalkeeper). In the training phase, the drill with 2 lines (7v5 + goalkeeper) is expanded to 7v6 + goalkeeper. The players have now completed almost 4 sessions structured around the soccer problem. We finish with a match-related drill (11v11). The coach can test whether the players have made progress.

Session 1
Development objective of the session
Session 1: This starts with a passing and shooting drill with the focus on forward runs. We then switch to a simple drill with 5v3 + goalkeeper, with the emphasis on getting the ball forward. We finish with a match-related drill (8v8).

Discovery phase:	Passing and shooting drill
Training phase:	Positional training (5v3 +K)
Game phase:	Match-related drill (8v8)

Content of the session
Discovery phase:
Passing and shooting drill

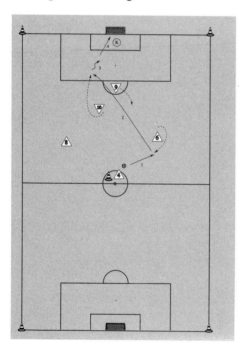

Organization:
Variation 1
- The defensive midfielder (4) passes to one of the other midfielders (6 or 8).
- The midfielder turns and passes to the withdrawn striker (10).
- The striker (9) runs toward the ball and the withdrawn striker makes a forward run.

Variation 2
- The defensive midfielder passes to one of the other midfielders.
- The midfielder turns and passes to the striker.
- The striker makes a forward run and the withdrawn striker runs toward the ball.

Variation 3
- The defensive midfielder passes to one of the other midfielders.
- The midfielder turns and plays a 1-2 with the striker.
- The midfielder shoots at goal.

Variation 4
- Free choice

Coaching points:
The defensive midfielder (4)
- Play the ball as far forward as possible to the right or left midfielder.
- Pass the ball firmly.

The right and left midfielders (6 and 8)
- Turn quickly.
- Receive the ball using the outside foot. This means that you are immediately well oriented.

The withdrawn striker (10)
- Ball forward.
- First try to draw your marker toward the ball.
- Try to get out of the field of view of the defender.
- Do not run straight forward but go wide first.

The striker (9)
- First try to draw your marker toward the ball.
- Make a sudden forward run.
- Do not run straight forward but go wide first.

Success moment:
X attempts at goal. How many goals are scored?

Training phase:
Positional training (5v3 + K) on a long, narrow field

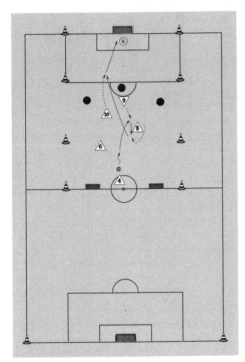

Coaching points:
The right and left midfielders (6 and 8)
- Look forward before you receive the ball.
- It might be necessary to play the ball with your first touch in order to send it forward quickly.

Withdrawn striker (10)
Forward pass
- First try to draw your marker toward the ball.
- Try to get out of the field of view of the defender.
- Do not run straight forward but go wide first.
- Try to anticipate what the midfielder will do.

Striker (9)
- First try to draw your marker toward the ball.
- Make a sudden forward run.
- Do not run straight forward but go wide first.
- Try to anticipate what the midfielder will do.

Success moment:
The winner is the first to score 3 goals.

Game phase:
8v8 (Depending on the number of available players.)
Free play.

Organization:
- We play 5v3 + goalkeeper on a long, narrow field (size depends on the action radius of the players).
- Attackers can score in the large goal defended by the goalkeeper.
- Defenders can score in one of the small goals.
- Offside counts.

Session 2
Development objective of the session
Session 2: In session 2 we continue with the drill 5v3 + goalkeeper from the previous session. In the training phase we then expand this to 7v5 + goalkeeper. The emphasis here is on how the attackers and midfielders combine. We again finish with a match-related drill (8v8).

Discovery phase:	Positional training (5v3 +K)
Training phase:	Line training with 2 lines (7v5 + K)
Game phase:	Match-related drill (8v8)

Content of the session
Discovery phase:
Positional training (5v3 +K) on a long narrow field

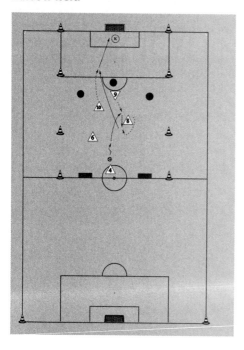

Organization:
- We play 5v3 + goalkeeper on a long, narrow field (size depends on the action radius of the players).
- Attackers can score in the large goal defended by the goalkeeper.
- Defenders can score in one of the small goals.
- Offside counts.

Coaching points:
The right and left midfielders (6 and 8)
- Look forward before you receive the ball.
- It might be necessary to pass the ball with your first touch in order to send it forward quickly.

Withdrawn striker (10)
Forward pass
- First try to draw your marker toward the ball.
- Try to get out of the field of view of the defender.
- Do not run straight forward but go wide first.
- Try to anticipate what the midfielder will do.

Striker (9)
- First try to draw your marker toward the ball.
- Make a sudden forward run.
- Do not run straight forward but go wide first.
- Try to anticipate what the midfielder will do.

Success moment:
The winner is the first to score 3 goals.

Training phase:
Line training with 2 lines (7v5 + K)

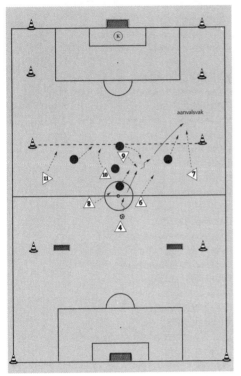

Organization:
- We play 7v5 + goalkeeper.
- The attackers can only enter the attacking zone by playing a forward pass.
- Only the wingers can cross the line with the ball at their feet.
- The other 5 can only enter the attacking zone when the ball has crossed the imaginary line.
- Attackers can score in the large goal defended by the goalkeeper.
- Defenders can score in one of the small goals.

Coaching points:
The right and left midfielders (6 and 8)
- Look forward before you receive the ball.
- It might be necessary to play the ball with your first touch in order to send it forward quickly.

Withdrawn striker (10)
Forward pass
- First try to draw your marker toward the ball.
- Try to get out of the field of view of the defender.
- Do not run straight forward but go wide first.
- Try to anticipate what the midfielder will do.

Striker (9)
- First try to draw your marker toward the ball.
- Make a sudden forward run.
- Do not run straight forward but go wide first.
- Try to anticipate what the midfielder will do.

Success moment:
A goal scored from a forward pass, without the opposing team touching the ball, counts double.

Game phase:
8v8 (Depending on the number of available players.)
Free play.

Session 3
Development objective of the session
Session 3: Here we return to the passing and shooting drill. The players now know the aim. In the training phase, we switch to the drill with 2 lines (7v5 + goalkeeper). We finish with a match-related drill (8v8).

Discovery phase:	Passing and shooting drill
Training phase:	Line training with 2 lines (7v5 + K)
Game phase:	Match-related drill (8v8)

Content of the session
Discovery phase:
Passing and shooting drill

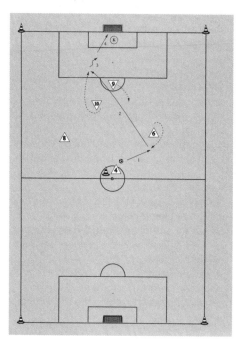

Organization:
Variation 1
- The defensive midfielder (4) passes to one of the other midfielders (6 or 8).
- The midfielder turns and passes to the withdrawn striker (10).
- The striker (9) runs toward the ball and the withdrawn striker (10) makes a forward run.

Variation 2
- The defensive midfielder passes to one of the midfielders.
- The midfielder turns and passes to the striker.
- The striker makes a forward run and the withdrawn striker runs toward the ball.

Variation 3
- The defensive midfielder passes to one of the midfielders.
- The midfielder turns and plays a 1-2 with the striker.
- The midfielder shoots at goal.

Variation 4
- Free choice.

Coaching points:
The defensive midfielder (4)
- Play the ball as far forward as possible to the right or left midfielder.
- Pass the ball firmly.

The right and left midfielders (6 and 8)
- Turn quickly.
- Receive the ball using the outside foot. This means that you are immediately well oriented.

The withdrawn striker (10)
- Ball forward.
- First try to draw your marker toward the ball.
- Try to get out of the field of view of the defender.
- Do not run straight forward but go wide first.

The striker (9)
- First try to draw your marker toward the ball.
- Make a sudden forward run.
- Do not run straight forward but go wide first.

Success moment:
X attempts at goal. How many goals are scored?

Training phase:
Line training with 2 lines (7v5 + K)

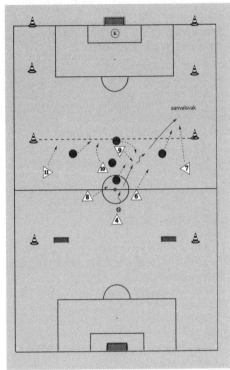

Organization:
- We play 7v5 + goalkeeper.
- The attackers can only enter the attacking zone by playing a forward pass.
- Only the wingers can cross the line with the ball at their feet.
- The team of 5 can only enter the attacking zone when the ball has crossed the imaginary line.
- Attackers can score in the large goal defended by the goalkeeper.
- Defenders can score in one of the small goals.

Coaching points:
The right and left midfielders (6 and 8)
- Look forward before you receive the ball.
- It might be necessary to play the ball with your first touch in order to send it forward quickly.

Withdrawn striker (10)
Forward pass
- First try to draw your marker toward the ball.
- Try to get out of the field of view of the defender.
- Do not run straight forward but go wide first.
- Try to anticipate what the midfielder will do.

Striker (9)
- First try to draw your marker toward the ball.
- Make a sudden forward run.
- Do not run straight forward but go wide first.
- Try to anticipate what the midfielder will do.

Success moment:
A goal scored from a forward pass, without the opposing team touching the ball, counts double.

Game phase:
8v8 (Depending on the number of available players.)
Free play.

Session 4
Development objective of the session
Session 4: We start the session again with positional training, but with an additional opponent this time (5v4 + goalkeeper). In the training phase, the drill with 2 lines (7v5 + goalkeeper) is expanded to 7v6 + goalkeeper. The players have now completed almost 4 sessions structured around the soccer problem. We finish with a match-related drill (11v11). The coach can test whether the players have made progress.

Discovery phase:	Positional training (5v4 +K)
Training phase:	Line training with 2 lines (7v6 + K)
Game phase:	Match-related drill (11v11)

Content of the session
Discovery phase:
Positional training (5v4 + K) on a long narrow field

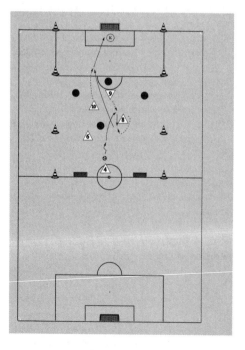

Organization:
- We play 5v4 + goalkeeper on a long, narrow field (size depends on the action radius of the players).
- Attackers can score in the large goal defended by the goalkeeper.
- Defenders can score in one of the small goals.
- Offside counts.

Coaching points:
The right and left midfielders (6 and 8)
- Look forward before you receive the ball.
- It might be necessary to pass the ball with your first touch in order to send it forward quickly.

Withdrawn striker (10)
Forward pass
- First try to draw your marker toward the ball.
- Try to get out of the field of view of the defender.
- Do not run straight forward but go wide first.
- Try to anticipate what the midfielder will do.

Striker (9)
- First try to draw your marker toward the ball.
- Make a sudden forward run.
- Do not run straight forward but go wide first.
- Try to anticipate what the midfielder will do.

Success moment:
The winner is the first to score 3 goals.

Training phase:
Line training with 2 lines (7v6 + K)

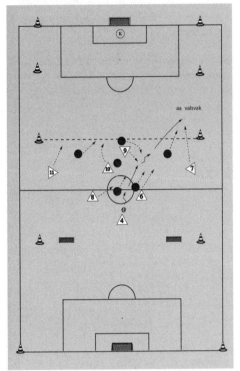

aa valsvak

Organization:
- We play 7v6 + goalkeeper.
- The attackers can only enter the attacking zone by playing a forward pass.
- Only the wingers can cross the line with the ball at their feet.
- The other 5 can only enter the attacking zone when the ball has crossed the imaginary line.
- Attackers can score in the large goal defended by the goalkeeper.
- Defenders can score in one of the small goals.

Coaching points:
The right and left midfielders (6 and 8)
- Look forward before you receive the ball.
- It might be necessary to play the ball with your first touch in order to send it forward quickly.

Withdrawn striker (10)
Forward pass
- First try to draw your marker toward the ball.
- Try to get out of the field of view of the defender.
- Do not run straight forward but go wide first.
- Try to anticipate what the midfielder will do.

Striker (9)
- First try to draw your marker toward the ball.
- Make a sudden forward run.
- Do not run straight forward but go wide first.
- Try to anticipate what the midfielder will do.

Success moment:
A goal scored from a forward pass, without the opposing team touching the ball, counts double.

Game phase:
11v11 (Depending on the number of available players.)

Task:
- The defenders put pressure on the ball.
- The attackers try to exploit the space behind the defenders and play a long ball forward.

Evaluation

Problem-oriented coaching

Have the players enjoyed themselves?
There was sufficient variation in the drills.

Has there been an influence on the soccer problem?
Progress has been made toward achieving the development objective:
- Improved forward passing to the striker and the withdrawn striker.

Is the number of practice drills in the training sessions limited?
There are a maximum of 3 drills in each training session.

Is the number of practice drills in the module limited?
A total of 4 practice drills are integrated in the module.

Is there a good balance between match-related and non-match-related drills?
Match-related drills predominate. The other drills such as passing and shooting support the match-related drills.

Is there a progressive buildup over a certain period?
Four training sessions are completed over a period of 3 weeks.

Are there sufficient repetitions for the players?
All players are sufficiently involved in each drill.

Is sufficient consideration given to the age group of the players?
The drills used in these practical examples are oriented to the players' age group. The content is adjusted to the age of the players.

Are the drills adjusted to their level?
The drills are applicable at the amateur level. If they are too difficult, the coach can easily adjust them.

Do the players have sufficient freedom of movement?
Sufficient free moments are incorporated.

Practice Drills

Passing and Shooting Drills

Passing and shooting drill

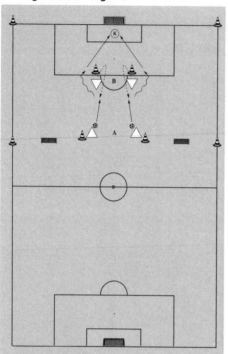

Development objective
1v1 with opponent behind.

Organization
Player A passes to attacker B, who turns and shoots at goal.
- *No marker*
- *Passive marker*
- *Active marker, who can score in the small goal.*

Success moment
Goalkeepers versus players. Players must score a minimum number of goals.

Coaching points
The attacker must 'feel' where his opponent is positioned. He can then assess whether he can best turn to the right or the left.

Attacker in front of goal
- *Check away*
- *Push off from your opponent*
- *Use both arms to feel where your opponent is positioned*
- *Keep moving*

Passer
- *Maintain eye contact with the attacker*
- *Play the ball away from the defender*
- *Pass firmly*

Tasks for the defender:
- Don't follow your opponent
- Try to get in front of your opponent

Passing and shooting drill

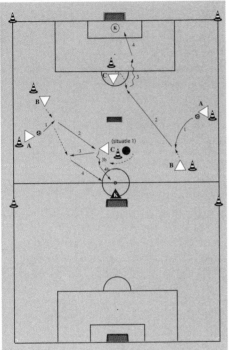

Vary the position of the striker: reposition the cone during the passing and shooting drill.

Development objective
Development of the technical skills of the striker (turning away, laying the ball off)

Organization
We work on 2 sides of the field. After the attacker shoots at goal he moves across to the other side of the field.
- *No opposition*
- *Handicapped defender*

Variations
A => B => C
C receives and variations
A => B => C => B
C lays the ball off to B with his left foot; B shoots
A => B => C => A
C plays the ball into the path of A. A runs with the ball to the end line and crosses to C, who shoots.
A => B => C (situation 1)
With handicapped defender beside attacker (when the striker receives the pass the defender first has to touch the cone)

CHOICE
Coaching and players' runs define the sequence
A => B => C
With active defender who can score in the small goal

Success moment
2 teams carry out the drill in parallel – which team scores 5 goals first?

Coaching points
A
- *Use your outside foot to pass the ball into the path of the attacker.*

B
- *Don't run forward too soon*
- *Use your outside foot to receive the ball*
- *Take the ball on the run*

C
- *Check away*
- *Use the inside of your left foot to receive*
- *Shoot with the other foot*

Passing and shooting drill

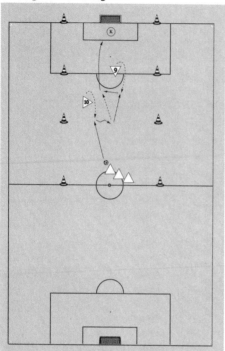

Development objective
Interplay between the striker (9) and the withdrawn striker (10).

Organization
Cones are used to mark out the zone. The players are free to move as they want to in the zone (striker with withdrawn striker roving in the space behind him).
The drills are carried out on the left first and then on the right.

Variations
- *The withdrawn striker checks away and receives a pass.*
- *The withdrawn striker turns and plays a 1-2 with the striker.*
- *The withdrawn striker turns and passes to the striker, who turns with the ball.*
- *The ball is played directly to the striker, who turns with the ball.*
- *The ball is played directly to the striker, who lays the ball off to the withdrawn striker*

This drill allows the players to express themselves. They take up positions relative to each other. This eliminates the artificial aspect of the passing and shooting drill with cones.

Positional training

2v1
2v2
3v2
3v3
4v3
4v4
5v4
5v5   Game drill

1 v 1 + K

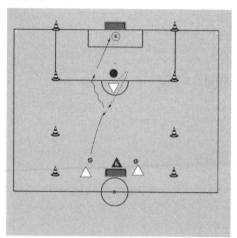

2 v 1 + K

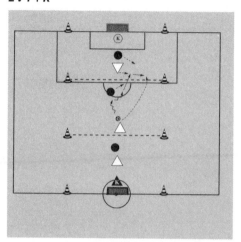

Development objective
1v1 with opponent behind

Organization
- *The attacker can receive the ball from either of the players beside the center circle.*
- *He can either lay the ball off or control it and turn.*
- *Change of attacker after 3 passes.*

Success moment
Who can score the fastest goal?

Coaching points
- *Feel where your opponent is positioned.*
- *Run diagonally toward the ball.*

Development objective
Interplay between the striker (9) and the withdrawn striker (10) in a 2v1 situation.

Organization
- *We start in the center zone with 1v1.*
- *The player who dribbles rte ball out of the zone plays 2v1 + goalkeeper with his team-mate.*
- *There can be one switch of flank.*

Success moment
Goals scored after winning the ball in the defensive zone count double. Which team is the first to score 6 goals?

Coaching points
Player in possession
- *Run toward your opponent.*
- *Options: 1v1, 1-2, or pass to attacker.*

Attacker
- *Check away diagonally*
- *Let the defender choose*

Switching between the attackers is stimulated unconsciously here.

2 v 2 + K

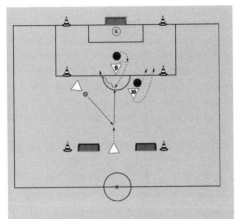

3 v 1 + K

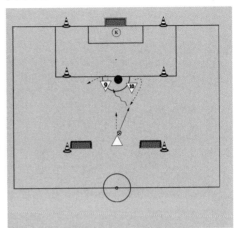

Development objective
Interplay between the striker (9) and the withdrawn striker (10) in a 2v2 situation.

Organization
- *We start with a mini passing and shooting drill. After the ball is played to the 2 attackers 2v2.*
- *The attackers can score in the large goal.*
- *Defenders can score by passing the ball back to A.*

Success moment
After the defenders score twice they become attackers.

Coaching points
- *Make space for each other.*
- *Don't always run straight toward the ball.*
- *Don't both go toward the ball.*
- *Exploit your teammate's run.*

Development objective
Interplay between the striker (9) and the withdrawn striker (10) and a supporting player.

Organization
- *In this drill, the player who passes the ball to the attackers joins in.*
- *Offside counts.*

Success moment
Goals must be scored. If the defender scores a goal, all the attackers must do 10 push-ups.

Coaching points
- *Force the defender to make a decision.*
- *Check away diagonally*
- *Get close to your opponent.*

3 v 2 + K

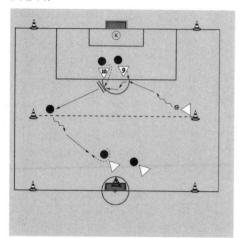

3 + K v 3 + K

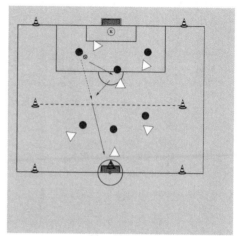

Development objective
Interplay between the striker (9) and the withdrawn striker (10) and a supporting player.

Organization
- The midfielder moves forward with the ball at his feet and passes to the striker or the withdrawn striker.
- The 3 players try to score in the large goal.
- If the defenders win the ball, they can pass it to their teammate on the center line.

Success moment
Which team is the first to score 5 goals?

Coaching points
- Try to escape from your marker
- Don't always run toward the ball.
- Call "free" if a defender leaves one of the attackers unmarked.

The drill can be expanded by introducing 2 wingers. This drill teaches defenders to pass the ball out quickly to the flank after winning possession.

Development objective
To encourage shooting from a distance and runs with the ball close to goal.

Organization
We play 3v3 in both zones. The player must not cross the center line.
They can:
a) shoot at goal
b) pass the ball to a teammate in the other zone

Success moment
A shot from the other zone counts double.
Who is the first to score 4 goals?

Coaching points
- Everyone must work together to get the ball to a teammate in space.
- Try to lose your marker.
- Try to create a shooting opportunity for a teammate.

This drill can easily be switched to 4v3. One of the players can join in in the other zone.

4 v 3 + K

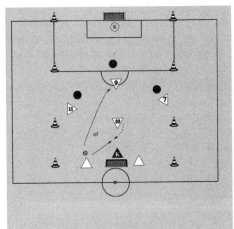

4 v 3 + K

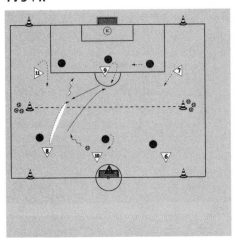

Development objective
Interplay between the striker (9) and with-drawn striker (10) and the 2 wingers (7 and 11).

Organization
Two players pass the ball around in combination with the withdrawn striker. The attack commences when the withdrawn striker receives the ball and turns with it, or another played receives a pass to his feet or to run onto.
- The attackers try to score in the large goal.
- The defenders try to score in the small goal.

Success moment
A goal scored after a forward pass counts double.

Coaching points
- Switch positions
- Try to play the ball to a player in an advanced position.
- Circulate the ball rapidly.

Development objective
Passing to the striker (9) and following up in support.

Organization
The field is divided into 2 zones. When the ball is played into the other zone a player can enter this zone (4v3). If possession is lost, he must return to his original zone.

Variation
A defender can also enter the other zone.

Success moment
When a goal is scored, the scoring team fetches another ball on the center line and keeps possession. Who is the first to score 5 times?

Coaching points
- The goalkeeper joins in the build-up (4 v 3)
- Play the ball firmly to the striker.
- Move up in support (third man).

This drill is mainly about passing to the striker. Use increasingly large goals with goalkeepers.

135

4 + K v 4 + K

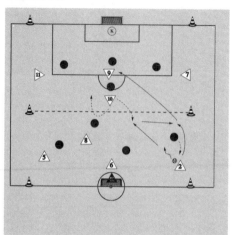

5 v 4 + K

Development objective
Interplay between the striker (9) and with-drawn striker (10) and the 2 wingers (7 and 11).

Organization
- We play 4v4 in each zone.
- The withdrawn striker or a winger can drop back to call for the ball.
- The player in possession can choose who he wants to pass to.
- Variation: The player who makes the first pass can join in in the other zone.

Success moment
Which team is the first to score 3 goals?

Coaching points
- Try to play the ball to the player in the most advanced position.
- Play the ball away from the defender.

Development objective
Interplay between the striker (9) and with-drawn striker (10), the 2 wingers (7 and 11) and a supporting midfielder (6 or 8).

Organization
- The drill starts with a pass to the withdrawn striker.
- The defender beside the goal joins in when the ball is played.
- We then play 5v4 + goalkeeper.
- The attackers can score in the large goal.
- The defenders can score in the small goals.

Success moment
1-0 for the defenders. Who is the first to score 3 goals?

Coaching points
- Depending on the position of the defender, the withdrawn striker can turn with the ball or lay it off to the advancing midfielder.
- If there is sufficient space, the ball can be played to the striker.

Game drill 5 v 5

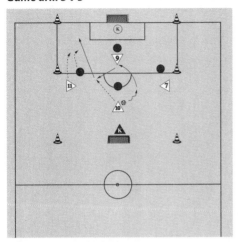

Development objective
Encouraging individual runs.

Organization
Free play.

Task
- *When the attacker starts a run with the ball, the defender must tap the ground with both hands before he reacts.*
- *You can give tasks to the attacker's marker. For example, try to get in front of the attacker when the ball is passed to him. This confronts the attacker with a different type of challenge.*

Success moment
A goal by the attacker, or an assist, counts double.

Coaching points
- *Try to shield the ball well.*
- *Use your body.*
- *Keep the ball away from the defender.*

Tip: Give the players time to experiment with the task.

Line training with 2 lines

6v4

6v5

6v6

7v6

7v7

8v7

8v8   Game drill

6 v 4 + K

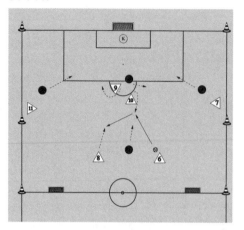

6 v 5 + K

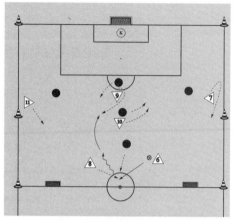

Development objective
Interplay between attackers and midfielders

Organization
This is an excellent basic drill.
- *In the center we create a 2v1 situation: 1 defender v 2 attackers.*
- *One of the attackers must call for the ball to be played to his feet. The other attacker is free.*
- *The 2 midfielders function as supporting players.*

Success moment
Three series are played. The first to score 3 goals wins.

Coaching points
- *Does the defender follow the attacker he is marking?*
- *Where is there space?*

In the second phase of the drill, a defender is positioned beside the withdrawn striker (6v5 + goalkeeper) and 2 midfielders are free.

Development objective
Passing to the striker (9), and the interplay between attackers and midfielders.

Organization
- *The striker stands together with the defender in a free zone.*
- *The midfielders play the ball to each other and take turns at trying to pass to the striker. A defender tries to prevent this.*
- *When the striker takes the ball, the free zone ceases to exist and we play 6v5 + goalkeeper.*
- *The defender must not enter the free zone before the striker.*

Success moment
All goals scored by the striker count double.

Coaching points
- *Maintain eye contact with the player in possession.*
- *Choose the right moment to run toward the ball.*

Depending on the level of skill of the attacker, the zone can be enlarged or made smaller.

Positional game (7v2)

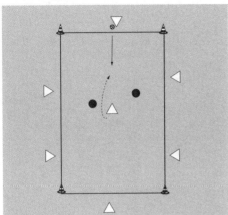

Development objective
Passing to the striker or the withdrawn striker.

Organization
- The striker can play as he likes.
- Lay-off players can pass to each other until the striker is free (1 or 2-touch play).
- 2 defenders mark the striker.

Coaching points
- Try to escape from the defenders.
- Keep making yourself available.
- Look for the right moment to pass to the striker.
- Play the ball away from the defender.

Give the defenders different tasks:
1) Defend close to the ball.
2) Close down the space behind the attacker.

7 v 6 + K

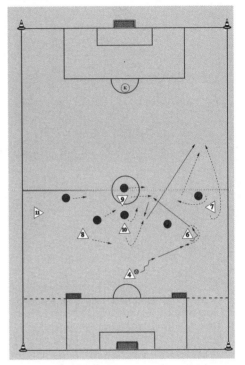

Development objective
Creating a scoring chance from your own half.

Organization
- Behind the area where the play takes place is a large open space (one half of the pitch). The team in possession tries to overcome the defenders (avoiding offside positions) and score a goal.
- The defenders can score in the 2 small goals. When a goal is scored, all the attackers must be in the half.

Success moment
Goals scored from a long forward pass count double.

Coaching points
- Patient build-up.
- Long forward pass when possible.

7 + K v 7

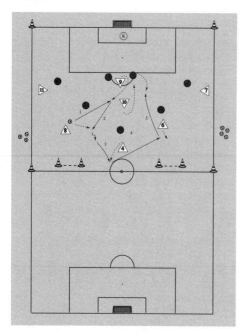

Development objective

Coaching the striker (9) and withdrawn striker (10) on how to combine; practicing technical skills.

Organization

- *We start with a passing and shooting drill with the emphasis on passing to the striker and the withdrawn striker.*
- *The ball is played to the striker, who lays it back. The withdrawn striker makes a forward run.*
- *The ball is switched to the other flank.*
- *The ball is played to the withdrawn striker.*
- *Once the withdrawn striker has touched the ball we play 7 + goalkeeper v 7 until a goal is scored. We then start again with a passing and shooting drill, but now from the other flank.*

The attackers can score in the large goal. The defenders can score by running with the ball through the zone.

Success moment

Attackers against defenders. How many goals are scored in 10 attempts? The attackers must score within 2 or 3 or 4 minutes. If the defenders score, we subtract one goal. Who wins the bet?

Coaching points

- *Where is there space?*
- *React quickly to the created situation.*

8 + K v 7

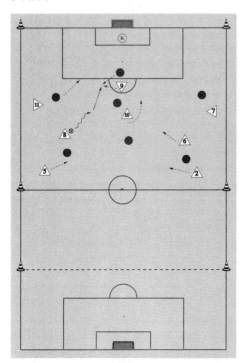

Development objective
After winning possession, rapid switch from defense to attack due to good cooperation between attackers and midfielders.

Organization
- *The team of 8 can score in the large goal.*
- *The team of 7 tries to play the ball in the zone and retain possession. The team of 8 tries to win the ball and initiate a good build-up via the striker and withdrawn striker.*
- *Offside counts when the ball passes from one zone to the other*

Success moment
If the team of 7 passes the ball 5 or 6 or 7 times in succession in the zone, it scores one point. If the attackers score, they are awarded 1 or 2 points (depending on their level of skill).

Coaching points
- *Fast ball circulation to create space for the striker and withdrawn striker.*
- *React quickly to the created situation.*

Depending on the level of the players, the playing area can be enlarged or made smaller.

Game Drill 8 v 8

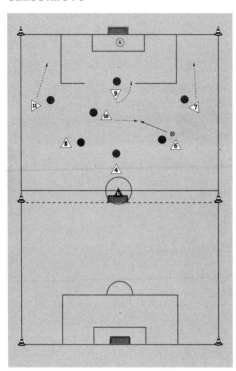

Development objective
Exploiting the space behind the defenders.

Organization
Free play.

Task
- *Objective: Improving forward play.*
- *Team A plays as far up the field as possible.*
- *Team B tries to exploit the space behind team A's defenders.*

Success moment
If the striker or withdrawn striker scores a goal, it counts double.

Coaching points
- *Fast ball circulation to create space for the striker and withdrawn striker.*
- *Try to get the ball forward as quickly as possible after winning possession.*

Take the predictability out of the drill. In the initial phase, tell only team B how to achieve the objective.

Line training with 3 lines

9v6

9v7

9v8

9v9

10v8

10v9

10v10

11v10

11v11   Game drill

9 v 6 + K

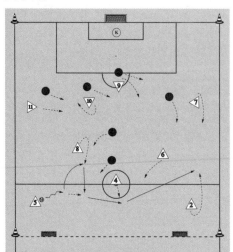

9 v 8 + 2K

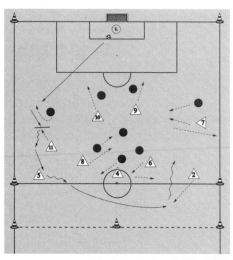

Development objective
Recognizing the right moment to play the ball forward.

Organization
- *The ball is passed round in a 5v2 situation.*
- *When the opportunity arises, the ball is played to the striker (9) or the withdrawn striker(10).*
- *The attackers can score in the large goal.*
- *The 6 defenders can score in one of 2 small goals.*

Success moment
The attackers must score 5 goals within 10 or 12 or 15 minutes. If the defenders score, we subtract one goal from the defenders' score.

Coaching points
- *Choose the right moment to pass the ball.*
- *Maintain eye contact when calling for the ball.*
- *Don't hold on to the ball for too long.*
- *Play the ball away from the defender.*

Task: the right or left back (2 or 5) tries to play the ball to the striker or withdrawn striker (the defenders are unaware of this task).

Development objective
Interplay between the striker (9), the withdrawn striker (10), the wingers (7 and 11), the midfielders (6 and 8) and the full backs (2 and 5).

Organization
- *The opposing team starts with possession.*
- *The goalkeeper plays the ball to one of the defenders of the team of 8. The other team tries to win the ball. When the ball touches the ground in the zone, the team of 9 tries to create a scoring chance via the striker and the withdrawn striker.*
- *The team of 9 can score in the large goal.*
- *The team of 8 can score by heading the ball over the imaginary line.*

Success moment
20 minutes – who is the winner?

Coaching points
- *Look for space in the opposing team.*
- *Try to win possession as soon as possible.*

The similarity of the drill to a genuine game is debatable. Winning the ball and then playing it in again is an unlikely scenario, and the positions of the striker and withdrawn striker are less predictable.

10 v 10

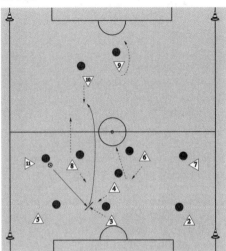

10 v 9 + K

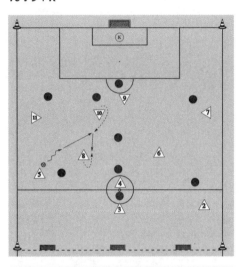

Development objective
Interplay between the striker (9) and the withdrawn striker (10).

Organization
- *8v8 in one zone and 2v2 in the other*
- *One team tries to retain possession. The other tries to win possession and play the ball to the striker and withdrawn striker in the other zone.*
- *When the ball is played to the attackers in the other zone, all the players move to the other zone except the striker and withdrawn striker of the other team and 2 defenders.*

Success moment
If a team plays 5 or 6 or 7 passes in succession in its own zone, it scores 1 point.

Coaching points
- *The striker and withdrawn striker must not move too soon toward the ball. They must leave sufficient space.*
- *You can call for the ball to be played forward or wide.*

This drill can be carried out with 2 large goals.

Development objective
Encouraging the striker (9) and the withdrawn striker (10) to make runs with the ball.

Organization
- *In the indicated zone, the striker and withdrawn striker can only be marked by their direct opponents. Outside of it they can be challenged by any defender. All players can run through the zone.*
- *The team of 10 can score in the large goal.*
- *The team of 9 can score in one of the small goals.*

Success moment
Goals scored by the striker and withdrawn striker count double.

Coaching points
- *Communicate with the attacker. If he can escape from his marker this opens up additional options.*
- *If you can, make a run with the ball.*

With advanced players, a limited playing area can be used. A zone can be placed in and around the penalty area.

Game Drill 11v11

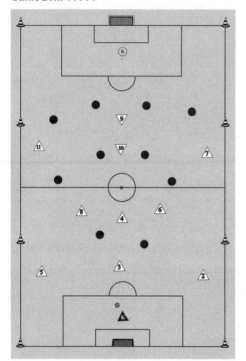

Development objective
How to handle the system of play of the op-position.

Organization
10 players and a goalkeeper play against 10 players and a goalkeeper.

Task
The opposing team plays 1-4-4-2 with 2 central defenders and 2 holding midfielders. The striker (9) and the withdrawn striker (10) find themselves between 2 midfielders and 2 defenders.

How do we handle this?
- Team A plays 1:3:4:3
- Team B plays 1:4:4:2

Success moment
Goals scored by the striker and withdrawn striker count double.

Coaching points
- Don't run with the ball too often.
- Act as a link player (from flank to flank).